Martial Arts

Mind & Body

Martial Arts

Mind & Body

Claudio A. Iedwab
Roxanne L. Standefer

Human Kinetics

Library of Congress Cataloging-in-Publication Data
Iedwab, Claudio A.
    Martial arts : mind & body / Claudio A. Iedwab, Roxanne L. Standefer.
        p. cm.
    Includes index.
    ISBN 0-7360-0125-5
        1. Martial arts--Psychological aspects. I. Standefer, Roxanne L. II. Title.
    GV1102.7.P75 I43 2000
    796.8--dc21

ISBN: 0-7360-0125-5   00-027092

Acquisitions Editor: Martin Barnard; **Developmental Editor:** Laura Hambly; **Assistant Editors:** Stephan Seyfert and Carla Zych; **Copyeditor:** Denelle Eknes; **Proofreader:** Laura Ward Majersky; **Indexer:** Betty Frizzéll; **Permission Manager:** Cheri Banks; **Graphic Designer:** Robert Reuther; **Graphic Artist:** Tara Welsch; **Photo Editor:** Clark Brooks; **Cover Designer:** Stuart Cartwright; **Photographer (cover):** Roxanne Standefer; **Photographer (interior):** photos on pages 2-3, 26-27, 56-57, 82-83, 106-107, and 130-131 © Roxanne Standefer; **Printer:** Versa Press.

The section titled, "Preventing Injuries," beginning on page 42 was reprinted and adapted, by permission, from Iedwab, Claudio A. and Roxanne L. Standefer. 1997. *Gorindo, Standard Manual.* Bancroft, ON: Sensei Uensei Books.

Human Kinetics books are available at special discounts for bulk purchase. Special editions or book excerpts can also be created to specification. For details, contact the Special Sales Manager at Human Kinetics.

Printed in the United States of America   10   9   8   7   6   5   4   3   2   1

Human Kinetics
Web site: http://www.humankinetics.com

United States: Human Kinetics, P.O. Box 5076, Champaign, IL 61825-5076
1-800-747-4457
e-mail: humank@hkusa.com

Canada: Human Kinetics, 475 Devonshire Road Unit 100, Windsor, ON N8Y 2L5
1-800-465-7301 (in Canada only)
e-mail: humank@hkcanada.com

Europe: Human Kinetics, P.O. Box IW14, Leeds LS16 6TR, United Kingdom
+44 (0)113-278 1708
e-mail: humank@hkeurope.com

Australia: Human Kinetics, 57A Price Avenue, Lower Mitcham, South Australia 5062
(08) 82771555
e-mail: liahka@senet.com.au

New Zealand: Human Kinetics, P.O. Box 105-231, Auckland Central
09-523-3462
e-mail: humank@hknewz.com

To Sempai,
who showed us the Way to carry on.

Contents

Acknowledgments

We are most grateful to Ruth and Barry, Rosemary, Naomi, and Richard Evans, who helped us keep body and soul together when we most needed it. Many others assisted along the way, including Jean Byers, Melanie Lord, Kathy and Sam, Joe Pach, and the patient ones among our students and stewards. Thank you also to Martin Barnard, Laura Hambly, Ginny Davis, Clark Brooks, and the rest of the team at Human Kinetics for their enthusiasm. Thanks to each other for being there.

Introduction

We can consider martial arts the original mind and body experience. Its traditions have roots in the teachings and practices of Zen teachers, samurai warriors, Shaolin monks, and those who interpret their true purpose as Art of Peace practitioners. Although you can practice many techniques without adopting the philosophies behind them, it is important to understand how these philosophies have influenced the development of the arts and the way we learn them.

Martial artists seek a centered, calm mind state that they can apply in active movement of the body. A mind and body integration that is both reactive and relaxed is the goal of the training. This integration isn't just about using the mind to influence the physical, or overcoming mental limitations with the body's strength, but fusing the two. Martial arts and other Eastern disciplines of health and healing do not subscribe to the Western view of a split, or dichotomy, of the mind and body. They suggest that it is the union of the energy of mind, body, and spirit that makes our world go round.

Definition of Kiai

In the Eastern view, the universe consists of energy called *ki* (Japanese) or *chi* (Chinese). This is the intrinsic energy of all living things. We can think of it as life force, internal energy, or spirit, but in a broader sense it relates to molecular and atomic energies, and in the body, kinetic and metabolic energies. For living things, it is a function of the air we exchange with our environment, the food and water we ingest, and metaphysically, the inspiration we develop from appreciating beautiful things and special moments.

It is our union with this ki energy, both internal and external, that is the purpose of martial arts training. In Japanese, the word for this union is *Kiai* (*ki* is energy, *ai* is union). Most people have heard of Kiai as the shout martial artists give when they perform techniques. This is a superficial definition of the word, being only the audible expression of the energy they are focusing using the mind, body, and spirit.

We all have ki. How we use it, generate it, concentrate it, and let it flow is the Kiai that distinguishes the athlete from the couch potato and the artist from the hacker. Developing Kiai, or working to unite the mental, physical, and spiritual energies, is not just one aspect of martial arts training but the entire reason for its existence as an art and a way of life. The techniques of fitness and self-defense are only methods and frameworks for learning and practicing Kiai.

It is important to distinguish between these uses of the words ki and Kiai, even though they are obviously interrelated. *Aiki* consists of the same two characters, and we sometimes use it interchangeably with Kiai. When discussing concepts derived from other cultures and expressed in different languages, we have to be careful of being absolute about the meanings of words. This is especially true when words have evolved from symbols, in this case Chinese and Japanese *kanji*, which represent ideas rather than literal translations of the components. Historical usage can influence meanings and be passed down by those wishing to illustrate ideas with the best word or phrase available to them. For our purposes, we will rely on interpretations of Kiai expressed by martial art masters in their own words.

We are choosing to use the word Kiai in a broad sense that includes the shout, the focus of energy for strength and direction, and the overarching interpretation of union of energy. We will use this term to describe a range of ways in which we can apply energy in the study of martial arts precisely because no other word exists that comes close to the ideas presented. Anyone wishing to understand the interaction of mind and body for their activities can use the principles involved and the concept as a whole.

Throughout this book we have used expressions from the Japanese language and traditions, for these are the ones we have adopted in our school of *Gorindo,* "the friendly martial art." Students of other disciplines such as *kung fu* (Chinese) and *taekwondo* (Korean) will find similar ideas expressed with different words. In America some have been anglicized and some dropped. It does not matter, because if readers are interested in the concept and what they might learn from it, they will be able to apply it in their endeavors.

The Meaning Behind Martial Arts

We recognize many approaches to the practice of martial arts. We can distinguish them by their goals and philosophies, which accord with the principles of their masters, who laid the groundwork in the past century and, in some cases, thousands of years before that. The practitioners who come to martial arts for self-defense, health and fitness, or competitive sport should realize that they are part of a great design—a way of thinking and learning that explores the relationship of mind and body. What students gain from the training will depend on what effort they make to understand all they experience on the path and on the quality of instruction and leadership they receive along the way.

Despite its popularity as a form of fitness conditioning, recreation, and self-defense, the study of martial arts is not by nature a casual activity. The student should bring a serious attitude and respect for the teacher and fellow students. There needs to be a basic acknowledgment of participating in a specific learning program, not just a sporting pastime or workout style. This places different demands on the teacher and student than what you might observe, for example, between a golf pro or aerobics instructor and those they direct.

© Roxanne Standefer

Through bowing, students show respect for their teacher, fellow students, and the art itself.

This emphasis on the way of learning is common to many artistic pursuits, especially those of Asian traditions, from which most martial arts spring. The idea of learning how to *learn* while you are learning how to *do* is an important contribution to Western sports and fitness cultures from the East. Unfortunately, some so-called martial arts schools have overlooked this. Too much emphasis on combat readiness or tournament achievement can miss the whole point of what martial art training offers. Of course this is not the easy way and therefore is less taken.

Martial arts demand intelligence. The student learns to think and analyze at length but also learns when to let go, to react rather than decide, and when necessary, to simply suspend disbelief until more data is available. Practice, practice, and more practice eventually reveals some basic truths. You cannot separate the mind and the body in martial arts. Although we learn to overcome fatigue, discomfort, and distraction by applying the mind to control the body, the body, through its responses to respiration, metabolism, and muscle relaxation, can also influence and direct the mind.

A good martial arts program is one in which everyone who is open to the instruction can participate in a supervised step-by-step fashion. There is so much to learn and enjoy that many will be overwhelmed if they are looking for the short course, the quick fix. The rewards are immense and long lived for those who try hard, practice well, and have a patient respect for the teacher. After all, teachers can only lead the way down the path they themselves are taking. When you are lucky enough to develop trust in a good teacher, you can avoid many dead ends, overcome obstacles, and explore interesting avenues.

Understanding and Applying Mind & Body Principles

In this book we will look at different aspects of how we regard the mind and body relationship in the martial arts, how we develop this relationship, and how we can feed back what we have learned into the training and our daily lives. None of these chapters exist as isolated parts of the training or its method of teaching; they reveal varied aspects of Kiai. Ideally these Kiai overlap and intertwine throughout the student's progress. The importance and relevance of these principles may seem to ebb and flow as they develop, but it is integrating their elements that will lead to the success of the martial artist in the practice and to the benefit to others who draw upon the wisdom.

None are left behind and none are moved forward before they are ready to learn the next lesson.

Those who might wish to dismiss these ideas and say, "Just teach me technique please," must realize that this mind and body relationship is precisely what martial arts training *is*. The exercises, the techniques, and the conditioning are just a way to learn about the subtle and vitally important principles that govern the practice. This is what makes martial arts so interesting and fulfilling.

The Eastern arts of calligraphy, painting, and flower arranging share with the martial arts similar philosophies and teaching frameworks. Although some might label this artistic categorization frivolous, meaningless, or at best not helpful in a street fight; the ancient samurai warrior, whose only goal was to serve with honor for his warlord, or *daimyo,* would practice these arts to focus his mind and energy, calm his thoughts, and perfect his technique. Without this understanding of deeper concepts, you have only punching and kicking, fighting for nothing. It is not martial arts.

People are now using these techniques (and the training behind them), which have been practiced for a long time and have amazed North American audiences in showy exhibitions, in high-level competition in sports, business management, and alternative medicine. The mind and body relationship is the latest trend in fitness and self-improvement movements. Yet martial arts professionals, in their imposed humility, have been slow to reveal the vast body of knowledge and expertise they can contribute to the discourse. This book will help martial artists, sports enthusiasts, and recreational athletes understand and appreciate the basis of these teachings. From this will come the tools to apply the lessons to other activities and endeavors, particularly those in which simple shortcuts are not enough and results are measured in long-term excellence and satisfaction.

chapter 1

The Learning Kiai

White is symbolic of the beginner's mind. It is pure, simple, and empty. It reminds us to always be ready to discover and to learn....

Tadashi
Nakamura

In martial arts, the beginning white belt wants to move like the expert, and the black belt wants to recreate the freshness of the beginner. Most people, young and old, get excited when they begin studying martial arts. They want to learn everything at once, train every day, and practice at home in front of the mirror. There is a powerful energy associated with learning something new; it makes people feel good about themselves and open to others. Although there is a lot to learn in the martial arts and it can seem confusing at first, the white belts are taking the first steps in the Learning Kiai—identifying a sense of self within their physical bodies and of the role their mental attitudes will play in the learning process.

The Learning Kiai involves a willingness to learn and an openness to what is being taught. Ideally it will be present at all times in the training process (along with other kinds of Kiai), but for the beginner it is all they have to work with. It isn't always easy.

The method of acquiring knowledge in the martial arts is structured. The beginner, intermediate, and advanced students have a special place and specific goals and responsibilities. In a good school, beginners are treated with respect, and although they may line up at the back of the class, it is so they can see and follow the movements of the advanced students ahead of them. Everyone was a white belt at one time, and the attitude of those who have moved further along the path should always be helpful and encouraging, never demeaning. After all, the only difference between them is when they first saw the poster in the street or the advertising in the phone book.

There is equal opportunity for those beginning the study of martial arts, and we measure progress individually. Everyone learns at different speeds, depending on their motivation, how much time they can devote to training and practicing, their inherent fitness level, and more important, their attitude about learning.

Respecting Martial Arts Traditions

Beginning any activity, especially with new people, can be a frightening experience. The martial arts, by their nature, their history, and their occasionally distorted reputation, can be intimidating to the outsider. An important part of the Learning Kiai for the beginner is summoning the courage for the first step inside the *dojo* (Japanese), *dojang* (Korean), or *kwoon* (Chinese), or any place, such as a community center, they have come to learn the martial arts. Newcomers have many questions. Their state of mind can be apprehensive, confused, or occasionally, overconfident to the point of being defensive and arrogant. Depending on what has motivated them to visit a martial arts school and the accuracy of what they know about the purpose of the arts, they may begin training with many preconceived notions. The martial arts have been around a long time, and it is better for the beginner to treat them with respect and to recognize that the traditions may initially be foreign to their understanding.

Differences in Attitude and Approach

If the heads of the schools view their way of life as a profession, rather than a business, they will expect the same in their students; that can sometimes be difficult for the modern Western consumer to accept. Although many schools in America promote themselves in the same manner as fitness clubs and offer similar amenities, some do not. There may be differences in attitude and approach. For example, one school may regard fees paid as tuition for instruction, another as membership dues in a club or moneys to support the facility. Rarely can an instructor charge what the true value of the teachings

An important part of the Learning Kiai is summoning the courage to take the first step into a martial arts class, whether it's held inside a typical modern dojo or in a more natural setting.

may be. After all, students will be learning techniques that could save their lives or the lives of those they love. Most people who stay in the training for a while state that it has had a profound impact on the quality of their lives. As students progress, their relationship with the school and with the teacher will change.

Schools will vary in their attitudes about the martial arts traditions. The head instructor, or founder of the style, will set the tone for how to interpret traditions and what changes to make to adapt to modern conditions or new research. It is important for the student to recognize that a healthy school is in a continual process of changing, learning, and adapting. It is a community, and its success is a function of the energy that the teachers and students bring to it. The teacher and senior students have many years of experience, and their methods may not at first be clear to the beginner.

An Open State of Mind

Addressing the training as a consumer rather than a willing pupil will produce a less than satisfactory result for the martial artist. The Learning Kiai will be difficult to achieve if students are demanding a particular service and are holding rigid views of what they are purchasing with their fees. Part of what makes martial arts work as a system for training the mind and body is a willingness to accept the relationship of student to teacher. The dojo does not work in a democratic process like a club or association. The tradition of the martial arts is transmitting knowledge from a long line of teachers. Students must be receptive and open to what the teacher has to offer, and suspend, somewhat, the expectations that they carried into the training.

The Japanese word for this mind-set is *nyuanshin*, and although we often refer to it as beginner's mind, this definition can be misleading. The term *shoshin* is a more literal meaning for beginner, but it is not the idea we wish to convey with the concept of the Learning Kiai. The image the ideogram *kanji* conveys for nyuanshin is one of a yielding heart, or softness. Most teachers will tell you that beginners, despite needing and wanting to learn as much as they can, rarely have that quality of openness and willingness necessary for true learning. Sometimes we have to break barriers before nyuanshin can blossom.

People rarely wish to be identified as a beginner, and in fact will go to great lengths to cover up weakness or error, but in the martial arts this label carries more respect and tradition than you might expect. In the East, a clean beginning, like the blank slate or white canvas, is an opportunity on which to build. Nonetheless, the term beginner's mind may not do justice to all that the concept of nyuanshin offers to the martial arts student. Indeed, any endeavor that requires a willingness to learn and an open mind can benefit from this idea. It is this union of process and attitude that we are referring to as the Learning Kiai.

This state of mind is what allows learning and progress to occur. It enables the martial arts practitioner to observe and understand the functions of the body, its physical manifestations, and the mysterious ebbs and flows of its energies. The martial arts teach that the communication between the mind and body goes both ways. If students are to learn how to coordinate, integrate, and eventually meld their operation into a smooth union of energy (the Kiai), they must listen and be aware.

Surprises, realizations, improvements, and solutions will often come unbidden in the process of training, and an attitude of nyuanshin will allow students to use them when they are ready. We cannot overemphasize the importance of this concept to the framework and philosophy of the martial arts; it is vital to understanding how the training works. It is the key to unlocking the complex relationship of the mind, body, and spirit. When you have discovered it, you can apply it to any aspect of your life to find enrichment and improvement.

Finding the Right Teacher

The role of the teacher is important in the martial arts. The teacher will guide the students through simple exercises that will shape their minds and bodies and help them discover the connections. Many martial arts traditions, which can appear on the surface to be merely cultural, are in fact basic exercises for the mind. Leaving your shoes at the door, carefully positioned for easy access, represents shedding the day's concerns and indicates a state of readiness characteristic of the martial artist. The experienced teacher can read an attitude by the way the students position their shoes outside the training area. For example, if a student is late for class and in her haste kicks off her shoes or forgets to place them on the shelf, or steps with wet boots on the raised platform intended for dry feet, or leaves smelly socks in her shoes to offend fellow students, these lapses will reveal much about the character of this student; similar patterns are likely to emerge in the training. The rituals of tying the uniform, or *gi,* and the precise configuration of the knot of the belt, help the student calm the mind and focus on the present, in preparation for the level of concentration needed in the class. There are many such examples.

Finding a good teacher and a school in which the student will feel comfortable training is an element of the journey itself. It takes a little time and research to discover who is teaching in the community and what styles and approaches they are offering. There is a saying that it does not matter which of the martial arts you study as long as you have a good teacher. This is generally true if the school follows a well-rounded curriculum inspired by the *Do* (Japanese, Korean) or *Tao* (Chinese). The Do is a fundamental philosophical concept that underlies and infuses much of Eastern thought, culture, and way of life. You can think of it as a journey, or more literally, the Way, of all things. It has a flow and energy like that of water in the manner of its passage on the surface of the earth and in the atmosphere as it circulates through all living things. In thought and in learning it is a guiding force for purpose and correctness based on what *is* and reflecting a natural order. Many artistic studies, including the martial arts, are Do disciplines; those schools that follow the Way are not just teaching fighting techniques and are not obsessed with competition. This is not to say that other schools with other priorities are bad, especially if they are honest about what they are offering and the quality of instruction is good. The point here is that to benefit from all the martial arts have to offer, particularly the mind and body connection, the health and fitness roots, and the self-defense prime directive, you must accept the *art* in martial arts, and the philosophical and ethical underpinnings of its teachings.

Students must examine their motivations and expectations when searching for a school and a teacher. As we have said, this is an important aspect of the Learning Kiai and is not just something that occurs at the beginning of your martial arts career. Circumstances will usually dictate that there will be more than one teacher to influence the student, and this is a good thing. Different perspectives, attitudes, and approaches benefit the student, as long as there is a balance between being open to other ideas and committing to one path for sufficient time to see where it is leading. It is easy to switch loyalties when the going gets a little rough, but you can miss the whole purpose of the journey. The martial artist learns to overcome obstacles with the knowledge already gained and some gentle guidance from those who have gone before.

The mind needs to be clear in these occasions, and the heart must be willing to have some faith in the experience and goodwill of the teachers. The ability to win championships or defeat the enemy does not always mean that teachers can be the most help to you in your experiences in the martial arts. Students must be honest with themselves, their fellow students, and

Students should strive to gain as much knowledge as they can from their teachers, while still remaining open to other ideas.

their teachers, and accept that they will change and grow as a result of their participation. Martial arts have always been as much about building character as strength and speed.

Learning for the Right Reasons

There are many stories associated with the history and traditions of the martial arts. Some have become legends and are strongly influenced by the philosophy of Zen, which uses fables and questioning *koan* (Zen riddles designed to bring a student past intellectualization to intuition) to illustrate, educate, and sometimes frustrate those who wish to follow its teachings. One traditional story is the turning away of the beginner who presents himself at the temple's gate, eager to learn all that he can, now. Although this is rare in the modern martial arts (replaced by a welcoming courtesy and perhaps influenced by a need to pay the rent), the school still has a responsibility to ensure that the prospective student wishes to learn for the right reasons. The head instructor must protect students from those who refuse to play by the rules and protect society from bullies and psychopaths who should not acquire skills that they could misuse to cause harm. We must take the practical application of the martial arts seriously. It is an important reason for the tradition of the direct transmission of knowledge from teacher to student and for some of the secrecy associated with its history. We often forget that the nature of what we study in the martial arts must dictate a more rigid ethical basis and structure than what we might find in other sports or recreational activities.

Another popular story is the one about the new student who asks her teacher how long it will take to become a master. In modern times the question is usually, "When do I get my black belt?" The answer, inevitably accompanied by a shrug, is, "It depends, maybe three to five years if you work hard." The eager pupil, keen to show her commitment will reply, "But I'll work twice as hard as anybody, you'll see! How long will it take me then?" The teacher, nonplussed, answers, "In that case, 6 to 10 years, I expect." The student, confused by this, exclaims, "No, no, you don't understand. That's far too long. I intend to train and train and fight and win, and I won't think or do anything else but martial arts until I achieve mastery. How long then?" The teacher, sadly having heard it all before, quietly states, "Twenty years then, or in your case, maybe never!"

A better question is, "How long do you train in martial arts?" The true answer is, "Until you die." This illustrates that studying martial arts is about more than acquiring a new skill or gaining another accomplishment to hang on the wall. The study of Do is a way of life, and if pursued with energy and discipline, it will offer rewards and experiences far beyond the simple pleasures of trophies and record times. This doesn't mean that everyone who begins training will continue forever or that someone shouldn't begin a martial arts class unless they are prepared to make that commitment. It merely points out that if you get on the path, find a good teacher, and apply yourself, you will discover a great deal more than you thought existed.

Gichin Funakoshi, considered the father of modern *karate-do*, remarked just before his death at the age of 89 that his only regret about nearing the end of his life was that he wished he had more time, because he was just beginning to grasp the true nature of the simple *tsuki*, or forward punch, one of the first techniques taught to the beginner. Such is the nature of reflection upon the physical by someone we can truly name a master of the martial arts. For those who need to know the answer quickly, it seems that the results of the training will take too long. For those who understand that the answer is not the object of the search, who instead use the whole self to keep alive the question and its genesis, the results are instantaneous.

When somebody wants something badly, perseverance and commitment will dissolve the barriers of difficulty and stretch the limit of the achievement. Unfortunately, in the mind of the unmotivated candidate, who gave up or was unable to challenge his entrance with sincere action from the heart, the clinical eye and experience of the teacher will never be clear. The teacher doesn't wish to make things difficult or to waste the time and effort of the prospective or probationary student. On the contrary, the teacher is ensuring that both will not waste them in the future. There is a lifetime of learning available in the martial arts and centuries of knowledge to explore. This is not a casual pastime, although for those who wish, it may serve as merely that.

Of course, beginners don't know this yet and, fortunately, in the martial arts no one expects them to. White belt beginners are in a privileged position within the system. They don't yet have responsibilities other than to show up for class; be respectful; open their eyes, ears, and minds; and try what the teacher suggests to them. It is OK to make honest mistakes or to not know what to do. Pretending to be anything but a white belt is not appropriate. The senior students won't waste much time helping show the way to those who are not sincere in their desire to learn.

Overcoming Fear and Frustration

Recognizing and cultivating the Learning Kiai is a challenge not only for beginners. As we will see in later chapters, it is an ongoing part of the program. It is mostly a function of attitude and patience, and in that sense is a process of the mind. Because the learning you must do is rooted so profoundly in the physical, however, the development of this Kiai shows itself in all aspects of technique, fitness, and endurance. Stiffness in the body often reflects rigidity of mind, for example, and until students learn to let go a little and relax with their abilities, progress can be slow.

Beginners come to the training with many fears, mostly about their capacity to perform and respond. The teacher needs to assure them that nobody is out to hurt them, that they will not be challenged to fight the black belts, and that they do not have to do their senior's laundry (all common misconceptions). Beginners still find it difficult to accept that their best effort will be sufficient and that no one is laughing at them. A trust in the teacher and a friendly, cooperative attitude in the dojo are important in making the newcomer welcome, but they are just as important for students at any level. Difficulties, challenges, and frustrations occur at many points along the path. If teachers do not present a method for accepting and overcoming them as a technique alongside the skills of blocking, kicking, and redirecting an attack, then it is not martial arts that students are learning, but merely fighting. It is of little use outside the arena of a confrontation and therefore is of little use at all.

Fears of the Beginner

Fear of getting hurt.

Fear of hurting someone.

Fear of looking like a goof.

Not knowing what to do.

Not being in good enough shape.

Not being flexible.

Fear of being afraid.

Fear of commitment, of not being able to stick with it.

Being too old.

Fear of the unknown.

Fear of the teacher.

Fear of the test, of performing in front of others.

Fear of being themselves.

Fear of confronting their demons.

Fear of choosing the wrong school.

Fear of wasting the teacher's time or slowing down the rhythm of others.

Fear of losing face when asking about something already explained in the past.

Don't worry about these feelings; they are natural reactions to beginning something new, especially something perceived to be challenging or demanding. The important thing is to see them for what they are so you do not let them defeat you.

Recognizing that these too shall pass with the training is half way to solving them. The other half is to follow the leader, and breathe, relax, and smile.

Overcoming fear or apprehension during the training is invaluable in dealing with stress, change, new situations, and other challenges in the rest of your life.

Learning How to Learn

Martial art is about learning how to learn and getting the most out of your existence in the universe. With this understanding, the student will be able to learn from many sources and distill what is important and useful. This ability will improve as the training proceeds and, as long as students keep in balance with nyuanshin, they will be able to accept more responsibility for their progress and to assist the teacher in helping others find their way.

Teaching Others

At advanced levels students recognize that one of the best ways to learn more is to teach others. This is a fundamental tradition of the martial arts and a keystone of the learning methodology. It is rewarding for students and critical for the functioning of the dojo; it allows the senior students to look at the training from a fresh perspective, analyze questions they might never have thought of posing, revisit the basics, and improve the accuracy of their technique in demonstration. Most important, they find out what they do not know and where their understanding is weak, unclear, or perhaps incorrect.

Exercising Patience and Maturity

Carrying an attitude that they have nothing more to learn or that they have mastered what they know is the death knell for martial artists. No matter what their skill level, practitioners with this condition will have more fear of showing mistakes than the white belt, and as a result their progress will stop; their interest will stagnate; and all the time, effort, and sweat they put into the training will be wasted. This can happen to students who have not embraced nyuanshin, and for whatever reasons, have not come to terms with their strengths and weaknesses in an honest way.

The beginner and expert must exercise patience and maturity, and enjoy their day-to-day progress. This is another area in which the traditional teachings of Zen and the Tao have relevance to the martial arts student. These philosophies can provide mental and spiritual encouragement and support for some intense physical challenges. The Learning Kiai has many components. Some are obvious and you can call upon them readily, and others are more subtle and elusive. Part of the teacher's role is to remind you of those elements you know and awaken you to the ones you don't yet employ. As we have discussed, having a positive and receptive attitude is one of the first and most important requirements.

The nature of the training is simple, but the ultimate path can be complex. It is sometimes difficult for the teacher or senior student to answer the beginner's questions in a direct way. This can be confusing for students, and they must realize that they do not yet know enough to be judgmental or to fit all the new information into their current mind-set. The Learning Kiai, to be effective, demands that students relax and enjoy the level of training they are at. This does not mean to always be content to stay at that level, but they must believe that through observation and practice, improvement will come. It is natural to not always comprehend everything that is happening. Most advanced martial artists will tell you that it can take many years before some questions are answered to their satisfaction. Usually it is not because the teacher hasn't offered a solution to a problem, but that the student has not yet been ready to understand.

Finding Satisfaction Through Training

Studying martial arts is fun and enjoyable. The breathing and exercise stimulate endorphins and other aspects of the metabolism to make you feel physically well, and the variety of new things to learn maintains the student's interest and excitement. An inspiring teacher and the camaraderie of fellow students can elevate the activity to a powerful force for positive change in your life.

An important element of the Learning Kiai is finding and keeping fun in the training. The practice isn't always easy. It can be physically demanding, and there will be times when you feel sore muscles and fatigue. With a good teacher and a little common sense on the student's part, these physical conditions will come from appropriate activity and be easy to recover from. Feeling tired from a good hard workout can be satisfying and productive. Good nutrition, rest, and the right attitude should result in an increase in energy and the desire to get right back to the dojo to train and learn more.

For the beginner one of the hardest things is to resist the urge to overtrain. A good program will insist on adequate recovery time for the body between workouts; this is also a time for the mind to analyze and assimilate the barrage of information it has experienced. In the same way that we are able to solve problems in our sleep and remember names or facts when we are not thinking about them, many subconscious processes occur during the downtime outside the training hours. The Learning Kiai can include this time when you are making no conscious effort.

The student must allow the learning to happen. This involves patience and keeping a sense of humor about your abilities. Most martial artists are surprised by what happens to them when they train. One common adage is, "Expect the unexpected." This applies equally to the samurai who lays his sword beside his bed before sleeping or keeps his chopsticks pointed away from the back of his throat when eating, as it does to the mild librarian who discovers the ability to break a board with a bare hand.

Teachers must encourage beginners to take pride and enjoyment in accomplishing seemingly simple tasks. Distinguishing left from right consistently and keeping your balance standing on one foot are extremely difficult for some, yet vitally important to the training. Such basic techniques are much more challenging than they appear, and it is common for many people, even those athletically proficient in other sports, to experience frustration. Learning to laugh at yourself and not at others is another important component of the Learning Kiai. As students improve, they will be amazed at what they have accomplished in a short time. As they look back and help the new white belts, they will remember their own first steps.

Benefits of Martial Arts Training

A safe, friendly environment for physical education and fitness.

A holistic, channeled activity for letting off steam.

Improved social interaction with peers.

Better focus and concentration.

Improved abilities at work or school.

Less illness and injury.

Better sleeping and eating.

Ability to defend yourself verbally, physically, and psychologically.

Avoidance of gangs, drugs, and excessive television.

Interest in other cultures, languages, and traditions.

A lifelong, interesting, and healthy activity.

Development of character and integrity.

Motivation for self-improvement.

Inspiration to perform responsibly.

Exercise of independent, deductive thought.

Training in solving problems.

Knowledge of the difference between training intensively and aggressively.

Development of a sense of justice, equilibrium, and defense of life and nature.

Enhanced coordination, confidence, and ability for other sports.

Measuring Progress

A good teacher and curriculum will lay the building blocks of accurate technique progressively, keeping tasks within the ability of the student both physically and mentally. Teachers must present new challenges as being in the realm of the possible, so the student will have a feeling of accomplishment at the end of the day. The Learning Kiai suggests that the student must be content sometimes with small increments of improvement. Martial artists concern themselves with their individual progress and do not look around to measure themselves against others. The training emphasizes that everyone has their own learning curve and that it does not stay the same throughout your journey on the path.

Colored Belt System

Many modern styles of martial art employ a colored belt system to mark the progress of a student through the ranks. In the goal-oriented Western cultures, we have readily accepted this structure, and people work hard to change their belt color through testing and examination sessions called gradings. However, it is important for the student to keep in mind that the colored belts exist to standardize the order of teaching techniques. For evaluation, the belts are not awards for accomplishments, but merely indicators of where within the system the student is working. When students change the belt color, it lets everyone they train with know what material they are now ready for, but does not imply that they have mastered everything that has come before.

This is an important distinction between the martial arts and many other sporting traditions and it relates to the culture from which they have evolved. In the traditional Eastern martial arts, there are often only white belts and black belts and sometimes a brown belt to indicate a candidate for the black belt examination.

In earlier times, when Japanese schools, or *ryu,* were organized around a single *sensei* (literally one who has gone before), students trained in the courtyard of their teacher's home or in the village square. They wore simple loose clothing, gathered about the waist with a sturdy belt of cloth, and although these garments were washed frequently, the belt became more stained with the sweat of exertion and ground-in dirt. The more students trained, the dirtier and darker their belts became. Senior students were eventually recognized by the color of their belt, but had no illusions that what they were wearing was anything more than a dirty white belt. When beginners learn of this tradition, they are less embarrassed by their white belt status in the class and look forward to the learning ahead of them.

Training Plateaus

Some students learn quickly at the beginning, then slow down as they progress. Others, who find themselves stuck going over endless basics before they can get a technique, will sometimes click at a certain level and start rapidly assimilating the material. Everyone must go forward at their own pace and expect fluctuations and plateaus along the way. This is why some teachers discourage competition among their students, feeling that it can impede progress and distract from the important lessons in the Learning Kiai. It is also why the colored belt system can be a valuable tool for the martial arts school if it allows students of different levels of experience to train together at the same time. The students do not have to worry about graduating with their class and will benefit from observing and being assisted by senior students. The advanced students have the opportunity in a general level class to

© Roxanne Standefer

When students of different levels of experience train together, it allows both beginners and more advanced students to observe and learn from each other.

practice the basics again and use these basic exercises, called *kihon*, to incorporate changes and corrections to their own technique.

Some students conclude that if they are not meant to compete with others, then they must compete with themselves. The Learning Kiai would add a barometer of caution to this notion. In the martial arts, as we've said, the learning proceeds on so many different levels at the same time that expecting an improved performance from one day to the next may be unrealistic. The Learning Kiai will involve periods of revisiting, reevaluating, and rebuilding technique and attitude. Even though you have not achieved or bettered a certain benchmark, you are still making progress. The martial artist must be prepared to break down to build on a firmer foundation. The humility, clarity, and confidence this requires are not necessarily born in your character; you must learn and practice these states. In this exercise of the head and the heart (or the mind and the spirit), the physical techniques become mere tools for building, shaping, and finishing the real work.

Skills of the Martial Artist

It is important to learn to work with a partner in order to achieve a better performance. Because much of martial art technique involves manipulating or avoiding another, this may seem obvious, but it is different to practice with an opponent than to learn with a partner in a cooperative way. There are two skills of the Learning Kiai that you acquire from working with another: sensitivity and observation.

Sensitivity

From the training point of view, it is vital for the student to exercise a high degree of emotional and physical self-control in order to be able to practice safely. If partners are accidentally injured during training, they will not be there the next day to work with you and will no doubt feel differently about offering themselves as human punching bags when they do return. Clearly, from a practical standpoint, this is ineffective.

In self-defense grappling techniques, we learn that the body moves only in a finite number of ways. Joints lock at a certain angle, and we cannot force them past that point without pain and eventual breakage. However, everyone has a different muscle mass, flexibility, and pain tolerance that will affect which technique to use when, for maximum effectiveness. The relationship of height, limb length, and weight will also be a factor in how specific tech-

© Ray Malace

The application of force in any technique requires a refined tactile sensitivity in order to avoid hurting or injuring your partner.

niques work. The difference in force application can be subtle, requiring a refined tactile sensitivity, both to be able to perform the technique at all, and more important, to practice it with partners without damaging them.

Part of this sensitivity involves staying focused and alert in practice in order to respond swiftly to the safety tap of a partner, indicating an immediate release of a technique. Most of the sensitivity required to train safely comes from your body awareness and concentration. Knowing your strength means paying attention to the details and staying in the moment. Daydreaming or showing off is unacceptable in a martial arts class for this reason. This is why teachers must design and execute curricula to ensure that students develop skills and qualities of character alongside technique.

Observation

The Learning Kiai develops powers of observation with all five senses, and by some accounts of Eastern medicine and belief, a few that are not among the five. Hand-eye coordination and the ability to pick up on the breathing patterns of an opponent are common examples, but it is more likely that heightened awareness and reflexes, and improved fitness (especially in the breathing capacity) create physiological and psychological changes that increase the efficiency of receptors and information processing. All humans rely on their conscious visual observation, but martial artists use all their awareness to anticipate an attack and respond appropriately. A good teacher will use a variety of teaching methods, including demonstration, explanation, and trial and error, so the student can observe and discover a range of responses when learning technique. Beginners will imitate and follow the direction of a leader. The leader must teach them to observe general movements and the fundamentals of stances, before worrying about hand positions and smaller details.

The advanced students, when learning something new, can perceive immediately what principles are at work and move accordingly. They can then focus on what variation or new manipulation the technique presents. In this way martial artists develop a repertoire of responses they can call on instinctively. Reaching this stage of advanced development requires a systematic method of learning, reflection and analysis, and, of course, practice, practice, practice. Without the Learning Kiai of the martial arts, this integration of observation and response will not occur.

Beginners must learn that by observing and correcting their reactions, helping their partners to do the same, seeing how the teacher assists others in the accuracy of their technique, and coordinating the mind and body they are embracing the Learning Kiai. Simple things such as placing the foot a certain way, keeping the center of gravity low, and aligning the head with the spine usually don't seem important to the beginner, who is eager to learn the fancy stuff. The advanced student observes these features first, knowing that having the basics correct provides the foundation for the more complex. A well-developed Learning Kiai enables the student to find enjoyment and satisfaction in recognizing the vocabulary of principles that become, through practice, the language of the martial artist's movement.

Attention to Detail.   Attention to detail is one hallmark of the trained martial artist. Distinguishing what is important from what is distraction is part of the training process. The teacher assists the beginner in making sense out of learning the technique basics. Students usually feel that they can't think of all the things they need to remember, all at the same time. If they get the feet and knees right in the stance, they discover that the left hand is doing what the right should do, or that they are holding their breath, or that they turned the wrong way to get there. With practice and guidance from a teacher, students will solve these challenges and movement will become more relaxed. The key is to build technique step by step, slowly and surely, with a lot of encouragement from the outside and patience from within.

Anticipation. Learning how to sense what another will do is obviously important in self-defense. Observing mannerisms, body language, breathing, and eye movement will assist the martial artist in anticipating an attack. Practice in sparring or *kumite* is an opportunity to learn patterns and indicators of how another person moves. Seeing the patterns in a partner helps you practice your response, both defensively and in counterattack, and helps you recognize patterns in yourself. Observing others is a key part of learning how to not telegraph your intentions to an opponent. Avoiding mistakes and learning economy of movement is the goal here, not proving yourself better than your partner.

Sparring is not the only area in which you can develop this type of observational and sense awareness. Training in group kihon or *kata*, with

© Roxanne Standefer

Training in group kata helps develop the awareness and response that is crucial in self-defense situations.

everyone trying to move at the same time and with the same energy, can benefit the sensitivity of the martial artist. There are obvious signal patterns, such as following the counting and watching when the person in front of you moves. Less obvious details, such as the intake of breath and the sound of a foot shifting on the floor, will assist the student in keeping in step with the class. With a little understanding and practice, you can see how to apply these details to self-defense situations. Eventually, the advanced student will feel rather than observe the shift of the eye or the flaring nostril, will absorb such data, and will integrate it with previous experience to produce fast reactions.

Accepting Correction. It is not always easy to correct your own mistakes. Some mistakes are obvious and some need to be pointed out to you by another. Even then we are naturally reluctant to accept correction, especially if we have not specifically asked for it. Being able to observe one's own technique while in the process of doing, and then being able to make the required corrections is a very useful skill in the Learning Kiai. Try to pay attention to the specific distractions, thoughts, or patterns that lead to errors. Generally with practice you will be able to perform combinations or patterns increasingly correctly, but improvement is always possible. Observe that when a new element is introduced, other aspects of the technique can "come un-glued" again, even after you think you have it "mastered." This is natural. When you are able to see errors, accept them, fix them, and move on without becoming frustrated, learning can continue and the Learning Kiai is rein-forced.

Martial artists will come to understand that this chosen path is about learn-ing how to learn, learning how the mind and body connect, learning how they feel about it all, and most important, knowing about themselves. On a fundamental level, martial artists will involve spirit, motivations, responses, and inspirations and make them available as resources. In the learning and improving process, students can alter these elements, strengthening or elimi-nating them depending on the needs of the situation and their personal training objectives. It can be liberating to discover that you can make changes in character. It is true that, with time and practice, you can achieve goals or dreams that you previously thought impossible.

Applying the Learning Kiai

- Listen to and accept the correction of your teacher or coach. They are making an observation from the outside that can be valuable to you. Don't waste time defending, arguing, or explaining.

- Relax about the speed of your progress. Everyone learns at different speeds and in varying patterns. Your speed and patterns will change as you progress. If you apply yourself, you will improve.

- Allow the teacher to be the teacher and yourself to be the student. Absorb rather than direct the lesson.

- Allow yourself to be surprised.

- Examine your motivations and objectives before beginning a new activity and occasionally during your learning process. Allow them to change. You may discover new and better goals.

- Do not be afraid to revisit and rebuild upon firm foundations, but stick with the path for a while before changing direction.

- Accept that there will be apprehension as a beginner and times when you feel that progress has slowed. Do not allow these building plateaus to prevent you from enjoying your activity at any stage. Anything worth learning is worth spending some time to do well.

- Be patient. Breathe, relax, and smile.

chapter 2

The Training Kiai

The purpose
of training is
to tighten up
the slack,
toughen the
body, and
polish the
spirit....

Morihei
Ueshiba

When considering the concept of the Training Kiai, we must remember that it is not a separate entity; it includes the Learning Kiai and other elements we will discuss later. For the moment, we can think of Training Kiai as the process of incorporating, improving, and maintaining what you have learned as new. Although you should maintain an attitude of nyuanshin, keeping open to new perspectives, the work within the Training Kiai is to develop a discipline for practicing what you have in hand and exploring it to the fullest.

Martial arts training is a method for improving physical fitness; learning skills for self-defense; gaining control over the mind and emotions; and concentrating your physical, mental, and spiritual energies into a unified whole. It is also, for many, an approach to intellectual and spiritual awakening. Its historic and philosophical roots offer a unique cultural perspective and a blueprint for holistic health. Although there are many mysteries associated with martial arts training, and varying viewpoints on what and to whom knowledge is revealed, there is only one real secret to its success: practice, practice, practice. It is here that the Training Kiai has its influence by ensuring that the student knows what and how to practice.

Proper Breathing Technique

A primary instrument in learning the relationship of the mind and body is the breathing mechanism. Breathing is both a voluntary and involuntary activity, meaning that we can decide to take a breath and determine how long we will hold it, but we can also forget about our breathing for a long time and the body will take over automatically. Our physiology responds naturally to the demands we place on it. Our respiration rate will increase when we need more oxygen and force us into a yawn when too much carbon dioxide is building up within the system.

Martial artists learn that breathing is a part of everything they do. It will affect their strength, stamina, timing, emotions, concentration, and vulnerability. The more control they can acquire over its processes and development, the better the results will be in all aspects of the training. Students should actively make the essential organic exchange of oxygen and carbon dioxide with the environment work for them and not react passively to its effects on the body. Looking closely at your breathing is the first step in body awareness and is fundamental to exploring the mind and body connection.

Meditation Exercise

One of the first exercises learned in a martial arts class is a short period of relaxed breathing and meditation at the beginning and end of the training session. In some disciplines this meditation is merely a quiet time to separate the class from the rest of the day, and relax the body and mind. Other disciplines place more emphasis on the philosophical and spiritual aspects of the study. We will be discussing the role of meditation more deeply in a later chapter, but for now we can examine the preliminary lessons as an exercise in breath control and mental focus.

Students sit correctly in the *seiza* position with feet underneath them or for more comfort with legs crossed. The more extreme lotus position favored by yoga practitioners is not as common in martial arts meditation. For many, the unnatural stretching of the knees can be destabilizing for other movements the martial artist requires. Even the traditional seiza position can be uncomfortable for beginners and affect circulation in the legs over long periods.

© Roxanne Standefer

Training sessions often begin and end with a short period of meditation, usually performed in the seiza position.

However, it is a good body position for the breathing and spinal alignment, and when practiced for moderate periods can improve the flexion of the ankles and the upper body posture. Traditionally, samurai warriors found it to be a sitting position from which they could rise quickly with sword in hand. At court no one could be higher than the warlord or daimyo, so attendants spent much time in this position. Individuals perform other traditional samurai activities in seiza such as the tea ceremony, brush painting, calligraphy, and flower arranging.

Students learn to tuck their buttocks in slightly and tilt the pelvis upward in seiza and later in stances and movements. This is partly for spinal alignment, but it also provides a structural sling for the abdomen and internal organs. Martial artists need to develop a musculoskeletal framework that will support their bodies and allow the muscles of the abdomen to relax and contract to control the breathing mechanism. In various exercises the students learn to visualize, isolate, and strengthen the diaphragm, a smooth sheath of muscle that separates the abdominal and chest cavities.

Abdominal Breathing

A martial artist breathes from the diaphragm or from the abdomen. This requires relaxing the abdominal muscles so the balloon of the lungs and chest cavity can expand downward into the upper abdominal cavity. This abdominal breathing allows a substantially increased volume of air to enter deep into the lungs. As a result, there is a greater efficiency of exchange of O_2 and CO_2 for every breath, because more alveoli (the small thin-walled air sacs surrounded by capillary blood vessels) are engaged. It also means that the respiration rate is lower for a given amount of oxygen intake and that you can lengthen the exhalation phase considerably. This is the same method of breathing that singers, wind instrument players, and swimmers practice.

Children and animals naturally breathe in this manner, but somewhere along the way, many adults begin to breathe only with their upper lungs. The chest rises and the shoulders lift when breathing moderately or even talking. In some cases this diminished potential is due to general inactivity; individuals never require the system to increase the volume of respiration beyond a base level that the lungs can easily and passively accommodate. Another factor is wearing tight clothes about the abdomen, which restricts the expansion of the chest cavity to upward and outward motion only. The Western view of fashion and beauty is an inverted triangle consisting of a broad chest or shoulders and a small waist. The Eastern view recognizes health and strength as coming from a low center of gravity, using the full capacity of the lungs with an expandable abdomen. Their triangle is base down. This is why sculptures of the Buddha have a happy, laughing belly, indicating a relaxed, grounded *hara,* or *tanden,* a point just behind and below the navel. (In Japan the term hara also connotes someone with integrity and emotional strength.)

In meditation and movement, martial artists concentrate and draw their energy from the hara or tanden. Students learn to focus their minds and breathing on this area for calming and strengthening. As an exercise in the seiza position, practitioners visualize the air naturally filling a vessel from the base in the hara and being squeezed out in a steady stream from the abdomen, like toothpaste from the bottom of a tube. The belt or *obi* of the traditional martial art uniform helps remind students of the location of their center.

Active Exhalation

Martial artists are stronger and more able to receive blows when breathing out and therefore seek to extend their exhalation phase as much as possible. The moment of inhalation is when you can be caught off guard, unbalanced, or have the wind knocked out of you. Students learn to breathe quietly and without visible movement of the chest. They also must to be able to contract the abdominal muscles quickly to protect internal organs and the nerve centers of the abdomen and solar plexus from a blow. The audible Kiai or spirit yell, aside from all its other functions, is a simple mechanism to forcibly expel air with a contraction of the abdominal muscle complex.

The student, by practicing breathing while sitting in seiza, learns to reverse a commonly held view of the respiratory mechanism. The traditional medical therapeutic practice views breathing as being passive in exhalation, with inhalation requiring the muscular effort. In response to signals in the brain, differences in atmospheric pressure, and the oxygen concentration in the blood, a person will take a breath by actively lifting the ribs to expand the chest cavity, thus drawing air into the lungs. By relaxing the chest, the ribcage naturally collapses on itself pushing the air out of the lungs. This exchange of air occurs primarily in the upper lungs only. In contrast, the martial artist trains the exhalation phase using abdominal contraction so it becomes natural and unconscious. In this practice the student slowly controls the outward movement of air and completely empties the lungs to a near-vacuum state. As you relax this state of concentration, air rushes quickly into the lungs without effort, filling them to maximum capacity from the bottom up. This method of breathing ensures that the lungs are fully emptied, avoiding a buildup of respiration by-products that can lead to fatigue or a feeling of breathlessness. In extreme exertion, martial artists redirect their minds away from the reflexive need to take in more air by gasping and instead concentrate on breathing out.

This method of breathing is efficient and economical and provides a high level of exchange, especially useful when you place heavy demands on the body for performance and endurance. Zen monks who practice breathing only, without any other aerobic or cardiovascular training, have been tested scientifically for blood gases, respiration rates, and ventilation capacity. The results showed the highest levels of respiratory efficiency and metabolic activity. We will discuss the intellectual and spiritual benefits separately, but keep in mind for now that, although we are talking about mental and physical responses and their causal and developmental connection, these elements are clearly interconnected. The martial artist trains to bring them into close harmony and direct control.

Aligning the Spine

The most important purpose of the correct position of the body is to facilitate the breathing, but all other aspects of physical performance including balance, energy, and natural movement will stem from this. In seiza, the student begins to work on aligning the spine in relation to the head and pelvis, seeking a relaxed but not lazy posture. The teacher usually asks the student to visualize a string pulling upward on the top of the head, from which hangs the plumb bob of the body. In practice, this position is a positive influence on elongating the vertebrae and relieves compression or misalignment of the spinal column. This is vital for the signal path of nerves along and from the spine to the lower extremities, as well as the circulation of energy and contraction of muscle groups.

The position of the head atop this structure will have an effect on balance from side to side and leaning forward and back. A small adjustment in the tilt of the head and position of the chin will influence how the upper cervical section of vertebrae are aligned and compressed. If out of line, the muscles and nerves of the shoulders, upper arms, and chest will compensate and possibly hold tension where none is desired or needed. A persistent misalignment can, over the long term, produce a problem in the lower back due to conditioned compensation. You can see here a further illustration of how small details can build into a larger picture.

The martial artist needs to develop awareness and control over these issues of breathing and posture. The student practices by isolating and visualizing the physical elements in the simple exercise of sitting quietly, before

In seiza, it is important to maintain a relaxed, but not lazy, posture.

extrapolating to the complex demands of the entire body in motion, where many things are happening at once. For the beginner it can seem too easy, even boring, to sit in seiza for long. The advanced students on the other hand are almost unconsciously running through a preflight checklist of their breathing, body position, center of gravity, and state of relaxation as they prepare for the demanding physical activity of the class. Mentally, the brain is eliminating the noise of distraction and tension and concentrating on each physical element of placement and balance to establish a flow of communication between the mind and body. As students advance, the energy of their essential spirit comes into play in the meditation exercise.

Developing Automatic Responses

This is the purpose of the Training Kiai, to forge these connections in the conscious mind, adapt and train them, then allow them to go into a modality like autopilot. Students must be able to retrieve these processes on command for adaptation or modification and be able to function without the mind, which they can free to absorb new information. Learning to let go is a major goal of the martial artist; in order to do so, physical responses must become natural and able to accommodate change.

Correct form and attention to detail in seiza are important so that later the mind can simply let go of detail. This is a profound principle in the Training Kiai, and although it seems contradictory to the beginner, it is part of the mental and physical training and must begin at an early stage. An example from traditional sources is a detail in the foot position in seiza. The feet normally are side by side, uncrossed, buttocks resting on the heels with ankles and insteps plantar flexed and flat on the ground. However, the big toes cross over each other, left over right. This tiny detail becomes natural when practiced and is an exercise in body awareness and the traditional self-defense preparedness. If an attacker were to sneak up behind the samurai in seiza and step on his feet, he would be easily immobilized and defenseless. The little precaution of the big toes lets one foot slide out from the other, thus allowing the warrior to recover from a disadvantage. This type of preemptive action is built into the training and practiced so it becomes second nature to the martial artist. It is an attitude of preparedness, mental calmness, and also defensive strategy. It is one small way in which practice of the martial arts reduces the necessity of ever having to fight.

The modern student of martial arts will want to practice this detail out of respect for the culture and the practical application of the traditions. Although it seems minor, it is important to recognize that this is a critical lesson in body awareness and attention to discipline. The students have to identify their left toe from their right, and cross them behind themselves without seeing, while lowering themselves to a kneeling position. Those who might resist this exercise as being ridiculous must ask themselves, if I cannot do this under controlled practice conditions, how will I learn to grab an attacker's thumb behind her back, and twist and turn, and direct my opponent to a fall as a defensive maneuver? Many who criticize traditional martial arts as being impractical are not looking below the surface of the training.

Under the stress of fear and shock, people forget much of what they think they know. Small details are the first to vanish from the available conscious mind. In the martial arts, centuries of training the human mind to live in a state of readiness for combat and survival have evolved techniques that are in some cases subtle and even mysterious. Nevertheless, they do work in reaching the subconscious mind and often result in awakening areas of the brain and spirit. Unfortunately, in the process of elevating martial fighting technique to the status of art, much of the reasoning behind the transmission of technique has been lost or distorted. Many aspects of martial arts training have come to be seen as artistic and are sometimes dismissed as impractical or mere window dressing. The advanced students find these secrets revealed to them daily and begin to understand the true beauty behind the discipline. When martial arts are elevated to the level of the Do, the many layers unfold like the petals of a flower, complex and simple at the same time. Every detail takes on importance.

From the details of extremity (i.e., position of toes and fingers, head and hips), the student works inward to more important but less visible physical elements of the seiza position. For the white belts at the beginning of their class, it is enough to gather themselves together, lower their bodies into seiza, find their center, and focus on their breathing. By counting a rhythm with their breathing, they practice to have the length of the exhalation longer than the inhalation and to empty the lungs fully. It can take a while to feel the abdomen expand naturally, but with practice, the abdominal breathing begins to take shape. Eventually the students will transfer this way of breathing into the pattern of everyday life and use it in the other exercises that are part of the martial arts training. In a gradual progression of technique complexity, students will learn to match their breathing with their movement and discover that their energy level and aerobic ability have improved.

As students advance, they keep in tune with their bodies though breathing and use the techniques of the Learning Kiai and the Training Kiai to develop their skill. Martial artists apply the principle of identifying, isolating, and alternately relaxing and tensing specific muscles, which they begin to learn in the seiza exercise, to every technique in their repertoire. Progressively, the body and mind work from major muscle groups and gross motor skills, to refining selective levers, pistons, springs, whips, and pointers, the fine motor skills of accurate technique.

Kihon Training

A major portion of the time that a martial artist spends training is in kihon or basic steps. As we have mentioned, these are not simplifications but foundation building blocks, somewhat like learning scales and arpeggios on a musical instrument. Once you have practiced these so they are strong, correct, and flow with smooth transition from one step to another, you can move from playing your instrument to making music.

Stances

Kihon training begins with stances. This is where the student begins to learn about weight distribution, center of gravity, and how to shift from one stance to another with balance. Again, attention to detail is important. The position of the toes and heels, the flex of the knee, and the orientation of the hips define the stance, and students must practice them until they become second nature. The Learning Kiai must provide the students with patience as they learn how to stand and walk. The Training Kiai will prepare them to dance.

The martial artist learns to build a technique from the bottom up. Stances differ according to purpose. Some, like the *kiba-dachi*, or horse-riding stance, are low and stable and intended for holding your ground. Others are for quick movement, or jumping, or extending your reach. No one stance is perfect or without some limitation or disadvantage. All have at least one angle or direction from which you can topple them, and often there is a weak point or aspect of the technique, which, if not done correctly, can cause injury or repetitive strain. This is why it is so important that the student accept correction and concentrate on accurate technique. It is also the reason a good teacher will not allow students to practice with full power or with such training devices as a heavy bag or *makiwara* (a heavy post anchored in the ground and wrapped with straw and rope) until they have achieved correct form.

It is easy for beginners to feel that such emphasis is not relevant to their purposes, and even intermediate students will sometimes forget the importance of solid stances as their minds become distracted by other details. Some will argue that most stances are useless and that the only stance of value is the fighting or guard stance. Again, only someone who is looking at the obvious and the easy makes this type of comment. The Training Kiai takes you below the surface to recognize the real purposes of the training, both physical and mental. Practicing the stances not only prepares the student to spring back from a fall or recover safely from a loss of balance, it also provides strengthening and stretching of the lower limbs. Martial artists recognize that because they practice deep stances in kihon, they don't need to supplement their training with knee bends or leg presses, for example. A good, well-rounded training program in martial arts does not require using weights or any external equipment. The back stance, for example, develops the position, muscle, and flexibility required for the roundhouse kick, the front stance for the front kick, and so on.

Learning to move between stances while keeping the center of gravity low and the spine in line with the head is essential. The head will follow the eyes,

Stances not only provide balance and stability, they also stretch and strengthen the lower limbs.

and the body will follow the movement of the head. Leaning too far forward or back will allow an opponent to easily unbalance you if don't fall over on your own. Individual body size dictates the length of stances and the distance between the feet, which reflect the mathematical relationship of the distance between joints. The physics of weight distribution, loads, and the structural principles of triangles, bridges, arches, and levers are all at work in the architecture of the body. Students learn what these distances are and can, with practice, accurately place their feet in the correct positions without thinking.

The proper linking of stances is vitally important to performing more complex techniques. Arriving at and leaving the stance with balance and precision is just as important as the stance itself. This is the body awareness that you acquire during the repetitive practice of kihon. Trained martial artists will sense invisibly the location and position of the body in relation to itself, its direction of movement, gravity, and balance. This is a step-by-step process, built over time as both a physical muscle memory and a mental construct that involves visualization, a sense of timing and rhythm, and a developed awareness of center, or hara.

Kihon Progression

Kihon training begins with simple exercises, usually just stances, performed with hands placed on the hips. This helps direct the attention toward the angle of the hips in relation to the direction of movement and properly aligns the body for balance and strength in applying force or resistance. When the student can successfully repeat the stances forward and backward across the training area, with consistency and relaxation, the teacher introduces turning. Progressively, the teacher adds basic blocking motions with the arms and hands to each step. The student is encouraged to be relaxed between movements and tense only those muscles necessary to hold the form. As the coordination becomes easier, the student can add emphasis to the moment of impact and time it to coincide correctly with the landing of the foot. Locking the muscles and joints to provide structural support to the block or strike refines the principle of relaxation and tension that develops as the student advances.

The Learning Kiai crosses into the Training Kiai when the movement or technique becomes natural. Mental processes evolve from thoughts such as, "which foot?" and "how far forward?" to observations of how the foot feels

© Roxanne Standefer

In kihon training you should only tense the muscles necessary to hold the form.

when it meets the ground and how smoothly the weight transition occurs. When the conscious mind has fewer detailed decisions to make, the student can group the individual musical notes of each aspect of a technique in a phrase that is smooth, long, and cohesive. It is these phrases that the student is practicing and forming during the kihon sessions, and eventually the mind can concentrate on the meaning and expression behind the phrases. For intermediate and advanced students, performing kihon allows them to focus on breathing, posture, flow of energy, and the joy of moving well.

Refining Basic Technique

Kihon is the workhorse of the Training Kiai. It is the vehicle for processing technical information, integrating technique with breathing, coordinating movements, and developing aerobic capacity and stamina. Participation in kihon is good exercise for every student at every level. Kihon offers beginners an opportunity to practice the basics they have learned through demonstration or discovery. The intermediate students practice the basics in new combinations. The advanced students enjoy kihon for the progressive complexity of combinations and work to smooth and refine their technique. Also in kihon students break down technique and analyze it for reconstruction and improvement.

Advanced techniques consist of fundamental stances and movements combined in new ways and with variations. Students usually learn them by adding each step, one at a time, or sometimes by the part and whole method. They practice smaller combination segments by themselves, then later stitch them together into a cohesive unit. When students need correction in a complex technique, it is useful to make the small correction as part of kihon practice, where they can isolate, fix, and reinsert it into the whole. In this way, they will incorporate the correction every time the basic technique reappears, such as in other combinations and in techniques where they may have overlooked it or masked it as an error. Often it is these small errors in a basic stance or a simple exercise that cause problems in executing more complex technique. This reevaluation is a continual process throughout martial arts training and is a distinctive aspect of its curriculum and method.

Mental Aspect of the Training Kiai

Training Kiai is not just about sweating and working hard; it is also about using your intellect to understand and analyze what and how you are improving your vocabulary of technique. Observing your mental processes and emotional responses to various demands on your body and enjoying the exhilaration when something new and awkward becomes comfortable and strong are as important as the dedication to the physical. Effort, energy, and persistence are attitudinal elements that the Training Kiai requires. The Learning Kiai, the thread of which must be present in all training sessions, tempers these elements with patience and willingness. It is this mental aspect of the practice that makes martial arts training so stimulating and sets it apart from many other exercise systems. You do not need to distract the mind to maintain interest in the physical program; in fact, the training demands its presence. The mind is participating in lessons, exercise, and practice goals alongside those for the body and makes corrections whenever it can. The goal of the training is the seamless integration of impulses, decisions, assessment, and a feedback modification of everything the body is doing. The Training Kiai, largely through the method of kihon, organizes and tests these responses systematically so that eventually they need not be under constant conscious control.

Respect and Attention

As we have seen in the Learning Kiai, correct attitude is an overriding factor in the success a student will have in learning and developing martial arts technique. When we consider all the benefits of the training in terms of health, character, and wisdom, we can see the importance of understanding the real goals of the martial arts system and how we achieve them. It is essential that the student realize and accept that this activity requires a commitment to ethics and safety in practicing and using the skills presented. The traditions and rules of good sporting behavior are supposed to cover the conduct of individuals in all athletic pursuits. But the martial arts, if practiced without due attention and respect for your training partner, could seriously harm someone. Students who become bored holding a focus pad for their partners could easily find that pad flipping into their faces, or worse, the punch or kick thrown at a wavering pad could miss and find a less padded target. Any techniques that involve contact or joint manipulation or that come close to a training partner's personal space require the utmost attention for safe training. At advanced training levels the exertion, fatigue, and effort, as well as the close contact with training partners, can arouse emotional responses that students must control well and keep in a training rather than competitive perspective. The standard of behavior and adherence to a strict code must be higher in the martial arts than in other sports.

If the principal attitude of Learning Kiai is one of patience and openness, that required of the Training Kiai is one of respect and attention. This attitude or state of mind is not only correct, from the point of view of being appropriate, but is also what makes these Kiai function at all. It is not the icing on the cake, it is the cake.

Safety Through Mental Focus

We have mentioned how some traditions associated with martial arts training have evolved to help focus the mind and address the practice in the right way. We will continue to see how these traditions are fundamental to learning the function of technique and how students acquire martial arts skills. Many methods and ceremonies have evolved to protect students from each other and themselves as they train. These traditions are as important in preventing accidental injury as they are in ensuring the integrity of the training and the art.

It is vital that teachers present techniques in the right order and when the student is physically and mentally prepared, especially in those arts involving contact between students, joint manipulation, falls, or weapons. Students, no matter how keen, cannot just jump in and flail around. They must learn to move smartly and safely before attempting risky techniques and situations. In fact, if adequately prepared, practicing with advanced students is much safer because of the discipline, accuracy, and self-control these students should have. This maturity involves emotional factors as well, and any negative attitudes of arrogance, aggression, or competitiveness must be nipped in the bud as unacceptable.

Training Etiquette

Many martial art traditions provide a structure to ensure that the mind and spirit are in appropriate relationship to the body and its activity. Bowing to your partner, shaking hands, standing and sitting correctly, addressing your seniors with respect, avoiding idle chatter and profanity, helping others, and being alert and present are all part of the integrity of the training process and help maintain the proper functioning of the school.

As physical contact increases, due to the nature of the technique or the intensity of practice, the relations between students become more formal. This ensures that everyone is paying attention and being careful, and leaves little room for tempers or misunderstandings to mar the training. The students must be able to trust their training partners to lend their bodies to the practice. Martial arts schools may sometimes appear militaristic in their discipline. This sense of order must not be confused or distorted to allow abuse or humiliation of students by others, and especially not by the teacher. Respect

Preventing Injuries

Before beginning any exercise program, consult with your physician about your current health and the effect of the activity on your condition. You must inform the school and the teacher of any concerns or cautions before training.

PROPER ATTITUDE

Training in a safe way requires the proper mental attitude.

- Maintain a positive attitude.
- Give the best of yourself and be enthusiastic during the classes and practices.
- Don't participate in the class if you are distracted, although a short period of warm-up and meditation before the class will help you find your focus. You can be a danger to yourself and to others if your mind is not on what you are doing. In this case it is better to sit out and watch the class.
- Ask the teacher if you have doubts or questions about a technique. The only stupid question is the one not asked.
- Be respectful, controlled, and appreciative with your practice partner. Be respectful with yourself.

PHYSICAL PRECAUTIONS

There are certain physical precautions that are vital to creating a safe training environment for yourself and others.

- Always begin with a warm-up and end with a cool-down.
- Always use a progressive increase of repetitions, intensity, speed, rhythm, and level of technique. Don't begin the class with your highest kicks or full power movements.
- Don't try to learn new techniques except under the supervision of a teacher. When working by yourself or with fellow students, work on improving the techniques your teacher has already taught you.
- Use correct technique and body mechanics.
- Maintain safety equipment, when required, in good condition.
- Ensure that your gi legs are above the ankles and tied high enough around the waist so they don't trip you or get caught up. Tie long hair back with a soft elastic; no metal or elastic clips, please. Remove jewelry.
- Don't be competitive during the classes; everybody has a different rhythm, level, and individual aptitude, although we do try to train in unison. Practice with instead of against. Don't feel compelled to better someone else's speed, intensity, or kick height. And don't show off!
- Don't sacrifice control of any technique for speed or power. Accuracy and ability to stop the technique midstream and not injure a partner (or yourself) is ultimately more important.

- Listen to the teacher's commands, rhythm, explanations, and advice. If the teacher suggests not kicking or refraining from further practice at the end of a class, there is a good reason to follow the advice. Don't spoil the previous hour of hard work by deciding to implement your own plan. Don't waste the sensei's time. Bow to experience.
- Don't forget that your activities outside the dojo will have a direct influence on your training. Other sports, personal training programs, diet, and sleep will strongly affect your body's metabolism and preparedness.

DEALING WITH ILLNESS AND INJURY

It is important to pay attention to your body and treat minor injuries to avoid having them become serious problems later.

- Be regular in practice. Don't try to make up for a missed week in one day.
- Don't overtrain. This can lead to illness and injury and eventually diminish your enthusiasm for training. We recommend that you take a day off between demanding training sessions. Let your body rest. This is when the most valuable strengthening takes place. If you are keen to learn, watch a class or read a recommended book.
- Do not train through pain. If you have an injury, make sure you give it sufficient time to heal. Consult with your doctor and teacher about modifications to your training. There are many therapeutic exercises that will help the healing process. Continued aggravation of even a minor injury can mean serious problems later. You can participate in many aspects of the class that do not affect the injured area. You can still learn a great deal by watching the instruction.
- Don't train if you are feeling sick. You will not only deplete your body's defenses, but also spread your germs to the rest of the students. The level of personal contact involved in the training is too high to tolerate this lack of consideration.
- Inform your teacher of any injury that may have occurred in or outside of the class and of any ill condition, doctor's treatment, or prescription.
- Train for enjoyment of your health.

will be earned, not demanded in a healthy dojo, and the students will learn that there is a time to be serious and a time to play within the practice. Students and teachers must always be vigilant for correct attitude within themselves. By having an accepted framework of etiquette that has meaning and purpose, you can readjust your attitude when necessary. This is crucial to enjoying the training but is also a vital link in controlling fear and anger when confronted with a situation in which you will need your skills in self-defense.

Knowing when to run, and when to stand and fight, calls for intelligence and honesty in assessing risk and ability. Keeping your cool and talking your way out of a bad situation requires a clear head and the ability to control your emotions.

Learning to breathe, relax, and smile in the dojo could save your life on the street. It will also make you a better friend, colleague, lover, and citizen of the world. You can learn what makes you happy and how to study that way. This is the goal of martial artists; they truly wish to learn potentially deadly techniques so they never have to use them. This is an art not easily acquired.

Individual and Group Activity

Training in the martial arts is both a solo and a group activity. The path is shared by many and traveled by others who have gone this way before. Nevertheless, the experience has solitary challenges that an individual must meet. The advice and guidance of a teacher and the helping hands of fellow students are part of the quality of the experience, and rarely can students progress entirely on their own. Fortunately, many teachings have been recorded in books, videos, and like materials and are available for those who do not have direct access to a good teacher. It is difficult though, to place a mirror in front of your integrity and character, never mind examining the details of technique in motion. The martial arts student who has a good training partner, a wise teacher, and a thoughtful curriculum is blessed and should make the most of the opportunity. The Training Kiai keeps the student on track through difficult moments and reminds the martial artist that following the Do is a lifelong vocation.

When students join a martial art school they accept, through nyuanshin and the Learning Kiai, that they will fit themselves to the training, not change the practice to suit them. This is harder for students training without a school or the direct supervision of a teacher, but it can be done. Martial artists accept responsibility for themselves inside the dojo and in their daily lives. We hope the training provides the tools to develop a balanced discipline and a way of organizing your mind to use the physical.

Warm-Up and Cool-Down

Every practice session must include some time for mental preparation and physical warm-up. As we have discussed, this occurs from the moment students enter the dojo, and we hope, before that in the students' minds as they make their way to the place for training. Changing into a uniform appropriate for the activity helps separate the practice from the rest of the day's activities and eliminates the trappings of status and lifestyle, so students can train as equals. What distinguishes them in the dojo are experience and knowledge, always with the understanding that they are to share it. Bowing when entering the dojo and the formalities that begin the class, including the seiza period, help bring the individual and group together in a good space and frame of mind.

The warm-up is essential to ensure that muscles and joints are limber and ready for intensive work. Never begin the class without doing these preliminary exercises, even if you are late. The warm-up is a time to raise the temperature of the tissues through increasing the blood flow and metabolic rate. Increased respiration and cardiac activity bring the body gradually from a resting, inactive state to one that can comfortably handle more vigorous demands. Once the muscles are warm, you can do light stretching exercises to gently loosen and bring the body up to speed. Full extension and power come later in the session when the body is ready.

After warming up, light stretching exercises will help prepare the body and mind for more intensive work.

This warm-up is for the mind as well. The variety of exercises ensures that the entire body is connected and that mental awareness of the state of readiness comes on line. You consciously coordinate the breathing with the movements by exhaling slowly and completely. Your mind returns to unite with the center of balance and energy in the hara with gentle movements and tuning the senses. Gradually, you increase speed and intensity and begin the practice.

After training, the cool-down period of light stretching, rotational exercises, and relaxation is as important as the warm-up. It will reduce the incidence of sore or pulled muscles and aggravated injury.

From Kihon to Kata

After the warm-up the student will often work through the drills of kihon basics. This continues coordinating the mind and body and brings the student to an elevated state of performance. A typical class may proceed from kihon to kata practice. Kata is a prearranged form that is more complex than the combinations repeated in kihon. It has a beginning and ending and can resemble a choreographed dance. The student approaches each kata initially as an exercise in the Learning Kiai. The teacher presents new movements in new combinations, involving challenges of balance, changing direction, jumping, and so on. The students observe, analyze, and build from the stances up to the fine details of the hands. Once students learn the basic sequence, the Training Kiai dominates the practice of kata.

There are prescribed moments for audible Kiai in each kata, and they help the students coordinate their breathing with the natural rhythm of the kata. Except in the learning phase, or when the teacher is correcting certain techniques, students perform kata with full effort and maximum control. Technique is conditioned by precise form and must be completely accurate. Performed by yourself or synchronized with the group, there is no improvisation or deviation from the blueprint. Yet even within this seemingly rigid structure, kata feels and looks like the most artistically expressive element of the martial arts training. Everyone is discovering and interpreting the true meaning inherent in the design of the choreographed work.

Students practice a kata over and over, as if polishing a fine sword or stone. Each time a kata begins, the martial artist has a new opportunity to do it well and enjoy the moment. Eventually kata can become a meditation in motion. For physical purposes, kata is excellent aerobic and anaerobic training, increasing stamina and strength quickly with regular practice. It is almost a complete form of exercise within itself, using every muscle and calling on

Kata can be a great way to increase strength and stamina and improve balance.

the body to perform bilaterally, isometrically, isotonically, and with full extension of the limbs and spinal column.

In some martial arts, especially those that involve grappling or throwing, students do kihon drills with partners. They practice the drills by breaking the technical sequence into parts, with each side knowing what the other will do. There are some kata that students perform this way as well, and the purpose is to finely tune movements and responses into a balletic pas de deux. Learning to relax and flow with the movement of a training partner is a fundamental principle of martial arts that allows you to anticipate and redirect the attacking energy of an opponent in self-defense.

Kumite

There are partner drills that involve blocking and striking, and these are preliminary exercises in preparation for *jiyu kumite* or free sparring. One- and three-step sparring (*ippon* and *sanbon kumite*) involve a predetermined attack by one partner and the choice of defense by the other. Students practice this repetitively in a formal fashion, beginning slowly at first and gradually increasing the speed and intensity until the responses are smooth and quick. The designated attackers will announce their intention to confront with an audible Kiai. The defenders respond, when ready, with their own Kiai, then the attacker steps forward with a punch to the midsection of the partner, for example. The defender moves away from the direction of the attack, deflects the blow with a blocking action, and finishes with a counterattack. At more advanced levels, the counterattack will not be just a returning strike, but could also include a takedown or restraining action that prevents further movement by the attacker. Also, the attack will change to techniques other than a simple stepping punch, making the measure of distance and timing more complex for the defender. Three-step sparring works in a similar way, with the attacker stepping forward and the defender retreating, blocking with each step and counterattacking on the final movement. The attacker can also vary the attack within the three steps as an advanced exercise.

Physical contact will vary depending on the technique, the skill level of the students, and the training philosophy of the school. The purpose of the exercises is to systematically introduce the element of choice and decision as well as the observation and analysis of an attack. Students practice ippon kumite over and over with numerous variations until they develop a vocabulary of responses.

With the practice of step kumite the body becomes increasingly accustomed to moving quickly out of the way and to deflecting and absorbing impact safely when necessary. The reflexes of the mind also improve with practice, so movements become almost instinctive. The student becomes accustomed to facing an opponent and sensing where and when an attack might be launched. The mind learns to record obvious as well as subtle movements of both the partner's and its own body, and learns to discern which motions are real and which might be tricks or diversions.

One difficult reflex for beginners to control is closing their eyes when something comes near the face. It is essential for self-defense to always know exactly where the attacking weapons, including fists and feet (or any other body part), are at any moment to move and block effectively. This is an exercise in body awareness and mental control over an almost involuntary reflex. It is another example of a small detail of physical and mental coordination that can have enormous impact on technique and greatly affect the outcome of a self-defense situation under stress.

Weapons Practice

Many martial arts styles and schools have evolved from completely unarmed systems. Historically, these ryu were developed during times of oppression or unrest when the possession of weapons was restricted to the warrior classes and those in power. In some traditional lines that use weapons as part of their training, common fishing and farming tools were modified into what today we recognize as martial arts weapons such as the *tonfa*, the *nunchaku*, the *kama*, and the *bo*. Martial artists practiced the techniques for using these as weapons in secret, and underground societies and cultures formed around their use and study. Some schools revolve entirely around the in-depth study of one weapon, particularly the sword, and some have even descended intact from warrior clans or families. In all these cases, though, weapons practice is used in martial arts as an exercise in focusing the mind and body.

Students train in the use of any weapon with the idea that it is a tool existing as an extension of the mind and not the hand. The physical adaptation and coordination required to wield a weapon effectively is considerable and almost unattainable without concentration, mental clarity, and relaxed flowing motion in the body. By practicing the manipulation of centrifugal and centripetal forces in working with weapons, and precise attention to detail, the martial artist can also improve other areas of technique and mental focus. When you see the weapon as an extension of the opponent's intention, you can understand why in defense you must take out the person, not focus on the weapon alone. Students learn an important lesson about the courage to step inside or move behind a frontal assault and are less fearful of a direct confrontation. They are forced to act with quick decision and determination.

Weapons practice is meant to be an exercise in focusing the mind and body.

© iPhotoNews.com

Integrating Mind and Body

Students practice kihon, kata, and kumite drills endlessly and under a variety of conditions. Their purpose is to fuse the mind and body so that reactions flow smoothly from perception through completion. Clearly, the body develops muscle memory and fast reflex times after many repetitions, but the Training Kiai seeks to eventually unite with the Meditative and Action Kiai to go beyond this state. The martial artist seeks a heightened level of awareness and readiness that almost eliminates mental processes and the time it takes for messages to travel to the brain. The senses perceive and the body reacts, without conscious thought, or at least at advanced levels it seems that way.

Amplified strength, speed, and pain tolerance also appear to be part of the integrated Kiai or Masters Kiai, the ultimate goal of training the mind and body. Obviously the Training Kiai is the foundation upon which other kiai can build. As we have mentioned before, the kiai do not exist in isolation. They are woven inextricably together and grow and flourish as a network does. Progress, in terms of expansion, does not always occur linearly or even geometrically. The Kiai can sometimes be viewed as multidimensional fractals with nodes that are powerful, lucid, and energetic. These moments when everything comes together can occur early in the training and seem almost magical to the student. They are usually short lived but exciting and satisfying when they do occur.

Students obtain a glimpse of the mental and physical state they are trying to attain and gain motivation to continue training. The classic problem here is that having once realized it for a brief moment, the harder a student will try to grasp that unique feeling again and the more elusive it will seem. This is when the student must learn to breathe, relax, and smile. Engage the patience of the Learning and Training Kiai, and practice with enjoyment. The rest will follow.

Kime

One way that students learn to acquire this integration of mind and body in a directed way, rather than having it take them over or descend upon them like a hallucination, is through the concept of *kime*. Kime is the maximum expression of energy in the minimum time, when the mind and body are focused in a single moment. Students coordinate a movement with the exhalation of breath, usually in an audible Kiai, with all the intention, energy, and effort they can summon from the hara. They focus the mind on the hara, and at the same instant extend toward and through that point in space to direct a strike; deflect a blow; or effect a turn, hold, or throw. The students perfectly relax the body and mind until the moment of kime, when they concentrate maximum tension, extension, or twist of the body (whatever is necessary), then immediately release it. The body and mind as one return to a state of relaxed form. By placing your whole spirit behind the effort, you access the union of energy that is Kiai and put it forward. By directing the focus toward an exact moment, that of kime, the period leading up to and away from that moment also becomes part of the concentration of mental and physical energy. This changing flow of energy is wavelike and controllable. With practice, this Kiai extends through longer periods and many different movements and combinations. Eventually martial artists are functioning at a high level of mental and physical performance and can draw upon a continuous cycle of energy, even though they may apply it externally only at particular moments and in appropriate form.

Relaxation and Tension

It is very important that the student always try to be aware of what is happening within his or her own body, mind, and spirit. Without becoming distracted, the martial artist in the Training Kiai tries to experience fully and embrace the action of the technique and the way the mind perceives the response of the body.

The principle of relaxation and tension is one of the most important to practice in the Training Kiai. It applies in every technique and is both a physical and a mental sensation; it is also what links the two. From the first bow through the seiza and warm-up exercises to the dynamic movements of kihon, kata, and kumite students are learning to identify which muscles to tense and which to relax when performing any movement or position. They learn to relax all parts of the body and mind that do not require expending energy at that time for that function. This allows martial artists to conserve energy, then expend it and concentrate it where they need it. The body moves better, the technique is more effective, and the mind doesn't get in the way. Obviously, this ability can take some time to accomplish and is an identifying feature of advanced students. Their movement seems effortless, yet strong and clean. Their faces and body language are relaxed and composed.

The Training Kiai allows the student to identify, process, and practice coordinating relaxation and tension in large and small actions. Repetition, good breathing, and a relaxed mental state will encourage the ability to move between these physical states so the response can become like a commanded reflex. Extending the relaxed state and minimizing the tensed state to only that which is necessary is a goal of the training. It is vital to effective technique, to a continual state of readiness, and to avoiding fatigue or injury in martial arts practice and in the demands of daily life.

The student must understand that relaxed does not mean lazy, sloppy, or without effort. The body is using correct form, and the mental state is one of alertness and energy, but the energy is not being wasted or confined. Similarly, the student must not confuse the tensed state with stiffness or hypertension and certainly not with drawing on aggression or rigidity in the mental processes. The appropriate relationship between relaxation and tension is a controlled dynamic that flows smoothly from one state to the other without damaging extremes.

Progress in the Training Kiai comes in many forms. On a purely physical level, the body will strengthen, flexibility and agility will improve, and stamina will increase. This allows the student to practice more often, maintain full intensity for longer periods, and enjoy the process of polishing technique and form. The mental benefits of accomplishing the exercise with greater ease and less thinking about correction encourage motivation and focus, and at the same time allow the body movement to flow in a more relaxed manner.

The effects of regular practice will vary considerably depending on the amount of new material introduced, the rhythm of the exercise, and the skill level of the practitioners. Nevertheless, it is clearly through repetitive drills and through kihon and kata practice that the work is done.

The Training Kiai is the center of the wheel for the martial arts student. When white belts ask black belts for the secret of success, they will usually smile and tell the new student to just go and train. This is not a dismissal but an honest evaluation of the situation. There are many twists and turns on the path, and streams that nourish along the way, but a simple commitment to taking one step at a time will usually get you to your destination. Focus on the step right in front of you for the Training Kiai.

Applying the Training Kiai

- Practice, practice, practice.
- Embrace the basics, never let them go. Practice them again and again to refine even the most simple aspect of your technique.
- Adjust your attitude to reflect changes in the mental as well as physical work. Prepare yourself to train well.
- Do not abandon the Learning Kiai when practicing what you know. There are still improvements and new ways that may require changes. Avoid practicing mistakes and reinforcing bad habits.
- Always make safety, injury prevention, and health improvement a priority over fitness, strength, and prowess. Never neglect the warm-up and cool-down.
- Approach each session and the training as a whole, progressively taking one step at a time.
- Beware of relaxation and tension. Ask yourself if you are using your energy effectively. Are you getting in your way?
- Practice, practice, practice.

chapter 3

The Action Kiai

The fusing of mind and body in karate is indescribably beautiful and spiritual.

Shoshin Nagamine

The Action Kiai involves fully mobilizing all the body's resources. The mind and spirit are fully engaged, producing a state of being that is alert, ready, and totally aware. The Learning and Training Kiai have brought students to the stage in which there is sufficient technique and fitness to move comfortably and apply themselves with accuracy and confidence. As we have mentioned, these moments of glimpsing the Action Kiai can come early in the training, and it is the goal of the teacher to provide students with such opportunities at all levels of the progression. As students advance they begin to understand that achieving the unique flow of energy, the Action Kiai, in all their movements is what the training has been about.

Although students can develop this state of high intensity through practicing kihon, kata, and kumite, it is primarily the latter two that allow the conversion of the deductive mental processes to the intuitive. Kata is a prescribed and formal presentation of movement, and kumite, at the other end of the spectrum, is mostly improvisational. Both require a vocabulary of techniques and a fluency in their use to access the energy of the Action Kiai. When students move forward with this background in place, they can make great advances in the training, and the day-to-day practice becomes fresh and invigorating again. However, the Learning and Training Kiai must still apply in problem solving, self-improvement, and protection against complacency as the student advances.

We should be careful not to confuse ourselves with the idea that the Action Kiai applies only when in motion. There can be moments of great stillness in the Action Kiai, but the body, mind, and spirit are still in a state of high potential energy, or readiness for action. Again, if we remember that no single Kiai is ever at work alone in the student's training process, we can visualize the Action Kiai as a fluid state, not just one in a progression.

Continuous Flow of Energy

We have discussed in the previous chapter the concept of kime, the maximum expression of energy in the minimum time. We can easily understand this as a focal point, a moment of concentrated effort around (usually) a particular technique. Each one of these techniques, like the Kiai shout that might accompany it, has an echo, a reverberation of energy that persists after the focal moment has passed. In a continued state of motion, these echoes overlap and, like a feedback loop, can build an elevated state of energy wherein the whole is greater than the sum of its parts.

This amplification effect sustains the energy of the martial artist in exertion and provides the inspiration to do more. In a practical sense, it also makes more power available for applying an individual technique or a defining moment. Concepts of physics such as momentum and feedback apply here, but equally important, on a mental and spiritual plane, are the words motivation and intention.

In Japanese, the word *mushin* encompasses all these aspects to describe this sustainment of energy and effort in a continuous flow. *Muga-mushin* goes further to define the devotion of all your spirit to a technique, with no thought of ego or results. This is a state in the Action Kiai in which conscious analysis or decision making is absent from the immediate process. In fact, the sense of the immediate is pronounced; we might alternatively view this as being in the moment, in the groove, in the zone, and so on. The past and future both contribute to and depend on the present but are not precisely part of it. This separation allows us to make the most of the moment we are currently living and offers the greatest potential for change, improvement, and maximum expression of energy. This is of critical interest and importance to martial artists. Once practitioners become aware of playing with this kind of energy, they also begin to define themselves in relation to the *art* of martial arts rather than merely the training process.

Developing Mushin Through Kata

The practice of kata offers the most opportunity for exploring and developing this aspect of the Action Kiai. Once students have learned the movements and form through repetition and the analysis of *bunkai* (the meanings or applications of individual combinations), they are ready to begin eliminating that element of brainwork from the performance of kata. There will still be times to rework, improve, and deconstruct the kata, but apart from these stages, there is another realm of practicing the kata in which different rules apply and students will obtain different results.

Again, those obsessed with combat or sport applications of martial arts training will not be able to realize these benefits and may therefore remain reluctant to practice kata. By not reaching beyond the Learning and Training Kiai, they miss much of the purpose of kata. Because of this resistance to open up and surrender to the spirit of the kata, it can seem impractical and not enjoyable. Kata, however, offers one of the few times when the student can practice with full speed and power, and as a result has great conditioning properties. Even kumite, which appeals to the less artistic and more pragmatic of martial practitioners, has specific limitations in these areas to protect the sparring partner from injury. Kumite tends to be choppy and erratic until practiced at advanced levels by true martial artists. Because of this, it does not lend itself as readily to developing flow and efficiency of movement as kata practice does.

Applying the Concept of Muga-Mushin

The martial artist practices kata over and over with maximum effort and tries to go full out. The challenge is to retain the finesse and exactitude that kata requires without holding back any energy or commitment. This is the area where muga-mushin lives. Students must execute each technique or combination in the kata with precision and passion for the moment in which it occurs. Without hastening to complete the current moment or shifting their full attention from the matter at hand, martial artists learn to project themselves so fully into the next movement that when the exact completion of the current moment releases them, they are physically drawn into the next as if sucked into a vacuum.

© Claudio Iedwab

When practicing kata, each technique should be performed with exact precision.

This is a difficult concept for the student to understand, much less put into practice. Moreover, like the exercise of not thinking of a purple elephant, when you are consciously trying to do it, it is difficult to achieve. It seems to require your mind to be in two places at once, yet in fact it requires the mind to be nowhere at once. By being nowhere, not fixed in time or hooked to any thought, the mind is able to be everywhere, relaxed, and aware.

When the mind is confident of the body's ability to rely on muscle memory, correct form, and application of forces, it is free to think less about these things and can enter a state of heightened awareness. It is then able to monitor the necessity for changes and adjustments, and to compute strategy based on sensory data and new information. At advanced levels of engagement in the Action Kiai, this processing becomes automatic and instinctive, and the body reacts to the perceived intention of the opponent even before he commences his action.

Clearly, this kind of mind and body dynamic is not something that occurs miraculously; students must prepare and nurture it. It is a state of being that students must practice to achieve and must practice within to be useful and effective.

Benefits of the Action Kiai

For the martial artist, the Action Kiai is a reward for all the hard work. Prolonged periods of training at this level can produce a near-ecstatic state of the body in motion. We can explain this as the physiological effects of oxygenation, the production of endorphins, and the other beneficial properties of good exercise on the human body. Beyond this is the synergistic effect of the mind, body, and spirit working together like a well-oiled machine, responsive, alive, and inspired. It is probably this property of the martial arts training, more than any other, that provides practitioners with the motivation to keep their bodies at a high level of physical conditioning and to practice regularly enough to maintain the coordination of the mental elements.

Part of this must be the psychological effect of being in control of your body and the confidence that comes from knowing how to draw on internal resources to perform well, both mentally and physically. Knowing how to defend yourself from attack and how to overcome difficulties using strength of spirit, and having the skill to focus or detach your mind when necessary also contribute to your personal capability.

The Action Kiai requires the good level of fitness that the Training Kiai produces, and it will continue to improve these areas of fitness: balance,

Kata Practice

- In the beginning, learn the kata from the sensei.
- Watch first, then do the motion.
- Learn the kata sequences in parts. Concentrate on stances before hand positions.
- Start and finish the kata in the same place.
- Keep the back vertical and the eyes looking forward.
- Always practice kihon; it is an excellent aid in developing good kata.
- Learn the bunkai.
- Know the method of learning and teaching the kata.
- Do kata with the appropriate rhythm. There is a rhythm for each kata that distinguishes it and is part of its character.
- Maintain positive spirit while executing the kata.
- It is not necessary to look fierce, merely calm and powerful.
- Kata begins as it finishes, with attention, bowing, and good attitude.
- You can train kata individually or in a group; in the latter case it is important to feel the rhythm of the other students.
- Breathe with the diaphragm muscle in every motion.
- Kiai has to be present constantly, but the shout, when the kata requires it, is the expression of the body, mind, and spirit working together in one action.
- The kime used while executing each movement in the kata is the maximum expression of your energy in the minimum time.
- Keep the balance of your body and let your mind relax.
- Feel graceful and joyous.
- Remember that kata gives us the chance to train an ample range of movements without injury to anybody. Because it is a fighting simulation, its realization conveys a control that expresses technical quality and energetic personality. An intention to do something with total focus and concentration, and an inner calm showing serenity and solid spirit, are necessary attitudes in self-protection.
- Through repetition and good practice, we can bring ourselves closer to the ideal expression of the kata. The ultimate goal of its practice is not the kata itself, but the harmony of the practitioner's character. Each time you execute kata visualize that you are polishing a valuable stone, smoothing the edges to get changes that bring transparency, light, and multifaceted reflections of the outside while retaining the integrity of the whole.

bilateral movement, breathing, cardiovascular exercise, coordination, dynamic motion, endurance, flexibility, harmonious muscle development, reflexes, relaxation, space orientation, speed, stamina, stretching, and strength.

Improvement will also develop in the areas of control of motion, defenses, dynamic action-reaction, fluidity, grappling, joint locking, kicking, knowledge of vital points, self-defense, strategy, strikes, throwing, and timing.

It is harder to define and measure the mental and spiritual effects of the Action Kiai than the more obvious results of the physical training. Coordination and fitness will come eventually to the student who practices, and you can readily observe improvement in these areas. We consider the same level of control and awareness in the mental, and especially the spiritual, phases to be advanced abilities. It is interesting, though, that these characteristics of the martial artist are the ones that translate readily to other areas and remain with the practitioner through periods of inactivity, injury, and into old age. Although hard won, these benefits are not easily lost and are the properties that allow a martial artist to recover quickly from illness or injury, or to fight on and endure extraordinary circumstances. Character development occurs along the following lines: adaptability, analysis, camaraderie, comprehension, concentration, control, determination, discipline, expansion of unconscious limits, focus, happiness, harmony, helpfulness, inner research, intuition, kindness, objectivity, patience, perseverance, politeness, respect, responsibility, social skills, and tolerance. The ability to improvise and survive in an emergency or tolerate the intolerable are defining characteristics of the martial artist and have led to the almost legendary stature of martial arts training. The magic that we pass in transmitting knowledge from teacher to student lies in unlocking and using the mysteries and the energies of the physical body, the complex mental network, and the human spirit.

In general, the Action Kiai is fun and liberating. It feels great to move and to reach and extend your limits. It is often the Action Kiai that reveals to students that they are capable of more than they may have believed possible. By engaging them in a state of high energy and gratifying accomplishment, they bypass or ignore many normal signals of fatigue, insecurity, and discomfort. Often students are surprised to discover that they have the resources to enable a second, third, or even fourth wind to sustain them. Once students learn that this is possible and acquire the will to speed up when the body tells them to slow down, the Action Kiai is working for them. The attitudes of the Training Kiai get them there, but the Action Kiai keeps them going.

Energy Control and Efficiency

The student learns that, when performing at endurance levels, it feels better to keep moving than to stop abruptly, and that applying a few well-placed verbal Kiai can direct and renew energy. In these periods, the martial artist must conserve energy by focusing entirely on correct technique, the principle of relaxation-tension, doing only what is necessary, and doing it effectively. The practioner should block, deflect, and avoid wasted motion, misplaced anxiety, and self-doubt as much as possible. In these moments the only thing that is important is the here and now, and the next small step.

The student develops this ability in practicing kihon and kata, in which movements are precise and controlled. Although kihon works from a steady beat or count, a well-designed kata introduces changes in rhythm, cadence, and timing. The practitioner has to find a balance in the breathing patterns and the muscular exertion to maintain the flow of energy and minimize fatigue. By relaxing the cognitive processes, achieved through repetitive practice and meditation, the body learns to perform well. The breathing will be able to maintain a smooth and long wavelength period that will unify the individual movements of a combination.

Timing and Responsiveness

The practice of kumite goes further in this area by introducing elements of choice in step kumite and eventually the randomness of jiyu, or free kumite. The primary function of kumite in martial arts training is to teach awareness and dealing with the unknown. The skills involve adjusting to different rhythms, syncopation within those rhythms, timing, estimating distances, and cognizance of surroundings. These are beyond the mechanics and execution of good technique. It is important that the teacher not introduce kumite too early in the student's development. There are mental and physical risks for a student who is not adequately prepared. Stances, joint positioning, balance, and concentration must be at a level sufficient to ensure the health and safety of the practitioner and that the practice of kumite has positive reinforcing value. Kumite is not a test of effectiveness or ability but a training exercise that should improve the student's skills and responsiveness. The attitude that you bring to a session of kumite will greatly affect the outcome of the practice and its relevance to your progress as a martial artist.

Minimizing the Risk of Injury

In kumite, as in kata and kihon, the Learning and Training Kiai must prevail in order for the Action Kiai to have its opportunity. The students must learn to have confidence in their ability to move out of the way or block incoming blows and must have control over their techniques to not hurt someone else in the practice. Even in those schools that do not involve contact, some errors or misjudgments of distance can occur. The student must be prepared to act to minimize risk and accept the occasional accident gracefully. When teachers instill in their students the skills and frame of mind that allow kumite practice to flow and be safe and fun, the Action Kiai will be invoked.

© Roxanne Standefer

Awareness and control are vital for minimizing the risk of injury during Kumite practice.

Learning From Your Sparring Partner

As in the practice of kata, students must gradually acquire the basics of blocking, movement, striking, turning, or (alternatively) grappling, throwing, locking, and pinning and then file these as useful tools. When the mind can view the large picture and when individual techniques combine into effective strategies, kumite will also provide the benefits and rewards of the Action Kiai. Clearly students obtain this more easily when their partners are well matched and share an understanding of the purpose of the training. When one student is at an appreciably different level than the other, the exercise is still valuable and should be enjoyable for both parties, but usually the Learning and Training Kiai are more involved than the Action Kiai. A good school and a responsible senior martial artist would never allow a session of kumite to be a monologue of blows rained upon an unsuspecting lower belt. Kumite is a dialogue between two people and involves the willingness of both participants to learn, practice, and exchange knowledge. In the case of a teacher working with students in practicing kumite, specific lessons might require shifting this balance to illustrate a principle, but the students must learn that this is a special case, not the way they should spar with someone else.

Adjusting to Different Rhythms

The student of kumite learns to move and adjust to different rhythms. Beginners tend to exchange one or two blows at a time in a regular beat, then let the other person have a turn. As students progress, the rhythms become more complex and varied, and they learn to syncopate their movements, that is, to move away from the expected beat and interject on the off beat. By changing from fast, repeated strikes to intermittent, for example, or striking when least expected, martial artists can throw off the concentration, breathing, and timing of their opponents. By controlling their reactions and being aware of flowing within their rhythms, martial artists can make kumite an extremely athletic dance.

Heightened Sense of Awareness

By observing their opponent carefully and fully using all their senses, students learn to anticipate attacks and prepare their responses. Their eye-hand coordination improves as the mind learns to estimate the distances and tra-

By maintaining rhythm and control, sparring partners can make kumite an extremely athletic dance.

jectories of movements. A keen awareness of their surroundings is a vital attribute of martial artists; this involves a combination of practice, calm mental state, and presence in the moment. The mind needs to be fully aware of all the signals coming from within the body and of the energies operating in a complete sphere encircling the body. Sights, sounds, smells, movement of air, heat, and cold can all give indications of danger. These impressions are important from the self-defense point of view, but they are also the stimuli that make our organism feel alive. The principle benefit of martial arts practice is the heightened awareness of your environment, and you should use this to experience life to the fullest. The Action Kiai allows us to breathe in and out with the energy of the universe and use it for our own purposes.

Perceiving Danger

The fully alive organism seeks to stay alive. The survival instinct is probably nature's strongest imperative next to the protective instincts of a mother over her young, which are similarly rooted. Nowhere are the mind and body so connected as in perceiving danger and responding to it. Fear and necessity can unite to drive the physical body to extraordinary performance, or in some cases, inhibit and freeze the mental capacities that control physical reactions. Martial arts training sorts out and controls the responses to potential or real attacks by having students practice the art of facing, confronting, and overcoming them.

An individual can unleash extraordinary resources when tested to the limit. Your perception of the challenge and your ability to meet it are ultimately more important than the actual situation in an extreme moment. Often it is not the physically strongest who survive but those who can withstand the mental pressures. Although there may be inherent factors in the ability to cope, martial artists believe their training allows them to improve and expand their abilities in this area. The Learning and Training Kiai open the eyes of students and help them progress through many stages in which they connect, hone, and tune physical processes and mental responses. This provides them with concrete examples in which they have overcome difficulty and turned situations around. As the tasks and challenges become progressively more difficult, they become more aware of what they realistically can and cannot do. However, as martial arts students advance and begin to use the energies of the Action Kiai and the stability of the Meditation Kiai, they also become aware of just how permeable the membrane between the possible and the impossible is.

Realistic Confidence in Your Ability

Although confidence in your abilities is necessary for you to achieve progress, overconfidence is a dangerous barrier to improvement. As we have discussed in earlier chapters, the ability to embrace errors and cheerfully correct them is vital to the progress of the martial arts student. Teachers who allow students to practice only in their comfort zone are doing them a disservice. These students may end up surprised by weakness or despair when faced with a real-life emergency. Martial artists know that they have triumphed over adversity in practice; even though they have experienced moments of failure as well, they have persevered, corrected their course, and made it over the rise. When they need to, when their survival is truly threatened, they will not only have this kind of experience to refer to, they will also have the vital energy of their organism to help them.

Fine Line Between Life and Death

This natural Action Kiai is a powerful mechanism that martial artists seek to access and control through their training. Partly fueled by the release of adrenaline and other related compounds into the bloodstream, the physical responses are clearly hardwired to mental processes. The profound psychological effects of crisis situations and the emotional impact of surviving accidents, attacks, loss of loved ones, or serious illness speaks volumes about the connection of the mind and body at these fundamental levels.

Some think that the precise psychological recognition of the fine line between life and death is what imbues martial arts training with its power and effectiveness. It is not hard to understand that the study of the martial arts is important from the self-defense point of view because it might save your life or that of someone you love. In a threatening moment, nothing will seem so important as your ability to perform some technique, or maintain your focus, or keep on keeping on. These threatening situations are life-changing crossroads in your experience. Those who are pulled back one way or another from the threshold between life and death are rarely the same people afterward.

It is this notion that inspired much of the philosophy, history, and legend of the samurai. Obviously, warrior cultures have in common a need to confront fear, danger, and the likelihood of their demise. Courage and resolve in the face of death were aspects of the heroic character, but training and experience could improve the ability of the warriors to keep their heads (literally and figuratively) and function under battle conditions. The preparation of the samurai, and traditionally the martial artist, is more oriented to personal protection than developing a soldier in an army. The motivations, ethical consideration, techniques, and strategy are different for the individual warrior and include many exercises and cultural references to train the mind and body.

Concept of Rebirth

Many poems, paintings, and stories have survived from the time of the samurai that deal with the appreciation of life and beauty in the moments before battle or committing *seppuku* (ritual suicide). *Hara kiri*, or self-disembowelment, was the method of choice for a samurai warrior to maintain his honor in the face of defeat. It involved an elaborate ceremony of precise motions and meaning, one of which was composing a death poem, usually in the form of a *haiku.* These words were highly valued, coming as they were from a spirit facing the threshold of death, and they were thought to contain clear vision and inspiration from such an experience. Those who for some reason were spared from death in the final moments of this ritual or even in battle were considered to be reborn and were expected to take up their lives as new people with different priorities and perspectives on life.

Martial arts training reflects these ideas in its overall approach to developing the practitioner. Certainly such threshold events as the black belt grading, for example, are significant stages in which a testing and renewal are offered to the student. However, the concept of rebirth is available in many smaller ways; it ideally exists in executing each kata, and, in fact, each technique. We have mentioned the image of drawing on a clean slate, but for some the analogy goes much deeper than that. When practicing, martial artists are consciously aware that their opponents have no intention of harming them. Nevertheless, their subconscious mind and the organism on an instinctive level recognize the situation differently. When, for example, the incoming fist stops one inch from the eyes, there is still a visceral response of the body and the nervous system, the primal responses to an attack. Martial artists are

© Roxanne Standefer

Threshold events such as the black belt grading can offer students a feeling of rebirth or renewal in their training.

seeking to open this window, to harness the energies within, and to benefit from the minirebirth that the spirit, mind, and body undergo as a result of their reprieve from perceived death.

Action Versus Reaction

Another aspect of the Action Kiai is the idea of the one chance or the one blow that can defend and end an attack. If you have but one unique moment in which to summon skills, power, and the correct assessment of the situation, then the spirit must be clear, the mind calm, and the body poised and ready. Action becomes the only reality; reaction may be too slow. Stopping to think is no longer possible. Analysis, reflection, trial, and error are activities that students must perform in practice with the Training and Learning Kiai. As a wise teacher often said, "Practice at home." When you absolutely must do it, it is the Action Kiai or nothing. We can also express this as do or die.

The flight or fight responses to danger are not intellectual actions of the mind. Nevertheless both the conscious and unconscious mind participate in analyzing the potential threat. At some point you make a decision and communicate it to the physical body, which reacts at the peak of its abilities. The goal of martial arts training is to explore this interaction and to fine-tune the response for self-defense in a modern world removed from the primeval jungle.

Mind and Body Health

The threats to our organism today are different on the surface, but we can find a rationale for maintaining a fighting trim and a comprehensive awareness of the danger lurking in our environment. Staying healthy is the biggest challenge to the human society due to stress, pollution, and sedentary lifestyles. Increasingly, Western medicine is coming to understand what Eastern health practitioners have preached for a long time: the mind, body, and spirit are intimately connected in maintaining health. In the cases of illness or injury, healing involves restoring the whole person to a state of balance, not just fixing the body.

Warrior Spirit

Psychologically, there appear to be many facets to the warrior spirit. Some of these, such as the need to win the battle, are more appropriate to the discussion of the Competitive Kiai in later chapters. For now when we speak of the Action Kiai, we are interested in the attitude and physical state that allow us to play full out for the sake of the play, not the eventual outcome.

Play Fighting

Play fighting, in its various forms, is clearly a dimension of human behavior that many species in the animal kingdom share. Most sports and games have evolved from war games played or practiced as training exercises, simulations, or celebrations of hunting or battle skills. Bears, elephants, lions, alligators, and insects, to name a few, all engage in play fighting and use practice sessions to teach these techniques to their young. Larger adult animals will fight gently with smaller, younger creatures and even go so far as to crouch or bend on one knee to bring themselves down to the size of their practice partner or pupil. Although the need to teach offspring the fighting skills they will require to live in their environment fits with the instinctive evolutionary demands for the survival of the species, it is apparent that the play fighting ritual provides more than a merely functional dimension in animal (and human) life. Adults will play among themselves, wrestling and batting each other about, but so too will animals of different species, sizes, and behaviors, if given the opportunity to interact. Many animals, including humans, seem to play fight just for the fun of it. Although some psychologists feel that these bouts are ways to establish dominance and social order, others suggest that we do it to feel good, release tensions, channel aggression, and sharpen our reflexes. Recently some analysts have linked the abnormal psychology of sociopaths with a lack of play activity and particularly play fighting in their childhood. A study of mass killers led one researcher directly to investigate the play patterns of animal species, recently documented by National Geographic.

Adaptability

Adaptability to changing situations has always been the hallmark of the survivor, for individuals and species. The ability to adapt implies a resiliency of the body, mind, and spirit as well as the strength and fitness to endure hardship. In the Action Kiai, martial artists are maximizing their potential to focus or concentrate all energies toward a goal, at a target, or along a path. At the same time, they are developing a hyperawareness that observes, experiences, and absorbs all the environment's input. Using the information and energy of your surroundings without being distracted from the objective requires a calm, stable center, high in energy, but not overcome or consumed by it.

To be oriented too outwardly is to be blown about by the changing winds; this is not adaptation but surrender. To enfold inward and steadfastly refuse to budge under your shell is to survive, but in a barren wasteland. The Action Kiai's imperative is to take action, direct the flow, and find balance upon the waters. This is where life and vitality can wield their power to change, improve, and stimulate growth in individuals and in those they come in contact with. This is the recognition that martial arts students must make: they *can* influence their destiny in the Action Kiai. However, they must first attain the skills, fitness, and attitude that they will need to function at this level and make the commitment to maintain them. Part of this is accepting forward momentum, to improve both physically and mentally to project a positive future. The balanced state will be one of stability in motion, in the same way that a bicycle rides, smooth and unwavering, when the wheels turn at a speed that overrides the effects of gravity, wind, or bumps in the road.

Generating Energy

Concentration, fluidity, reaction, and response are the operative characteristics of the Action Kiai. Uniting the energy available and using it efficiently feels like you have *created* energy, and although this is theorized to be impossible, we readily accept the concept of generating or converting energy the way we harness hydroelectric power from the flow of a river.

Avoiding Aggression

The Action Kiai is an evolved state that is akin to joy. To go for the joy in your training means more than to laugh and have fun, although you will do these things when appropriate. To unleash physical and spiritual energies and circulate ki freely, you must have no barriers or blockages. At the same time you must have a clear course to follow. This is why it is counterproductive for students to practice with aggression or anger in their minds, for although there are certain energies associated with such emotions, they cloud and distort correct action and thought. Martial artists believe that they can access the fundamental energies of self-preservation in more direct ways without the side effects of these negative feelings. Although anger may seem to work in the moment to achieve an objective, the person is usually left with exhaustion, resentment, and a draining of ki. There is no union of energy, only frustration with the situation. From a training point of view, the effects of aggressive attitudes on fellow students and training partners is similarly destructive and soon leads to a breakdown in cooperation and morale. This is also an environment in which accidents can happen and the productive development of character and spirit does not occur.

Immediately obvious is that it is much more enjoyable to participate in an activity in which the attitude is one of improvement, learning, and positive reinforcement than one in which you must constantly carry the baggage of negative emotions.

What is the point of learning to protect yourself from attack if you bring the associated elements of fear, anger, and hatred directly into your training area with you? Where can you escape and live happily? Most martial artists will tell you that they can sense the vibration of someone who is operating from a negative point of view. In the training this vibe is magnified and becomes disruptive to the process. This is why good schools and teachers work so hard to maintain a positive environment and an emphasis on correct attitude. The training demands the discipline to always bring your best foot forward. It reinforces the traditions and philosophies. The strict etiquette of the dojo helps maintain decorum when tempers might flare or misunderstandings occur. The results for the individual and the group in terms of health and happiness prove the necessity of incorporating mental and spiritual teaching along with the physical techniques.

Readiness

To be adaptable also means to be ready for action. Although circumstances in which you must defend yourself with physical force are rare, they do occur. Martial arts training teaches individuals to avoid or defuse such situations but also prepares them to respond if necessary. Self-defense is the reason many people join a martial art school in the first place, but many who continue with the training begin to see that the techniques are only one aspect of the practice. The mental attitude of being prepared and the ability to engage the physical body to survive a confrontation are just as important.

We have mentioned how the practice of step sparring or kumite systematically prepares the student to respond to an attack. By isolating the elements and practicing them until they become a smooth whole, the student becomes less intimidated by the idea of dealing with a confrontation. The martial artist is taught to expect the unexpected. This idea recognizes the need to stay in the moment and be aware of what is really happening, not just what you think will happen. It teaches students to learn from experience but not be locked into what has happened before or how they have always responded to a situation. By extension, you can see that, strategically, the martial artist must do the unexpected to gain the upper hand.

Martial arts training teaches you how to be mentally and physically prepared should a real self-defense situation such as a knife attack ever occur.

In the Action Kiai, the ready and the active states are not inwardly different, although the outward manifestations appear to be so. In terms of being prepared, any mental visualization of how to respond should be a calm reproduction of the training process and provide the blueprint for the reactions in a real situation. The more training students have, the more able to exercise continuity in mental attitude and physical response they should be. Ideally the spiritual self remains unruffled and centered. After all it is the *center,* where the soul dwells, that we are trying hardest to protect from harm.

Street Confrontations

With this image we can see how the martial artist can continue and recover when injured and also how self-defense applies to more than protection from the proverbial attacker in the dark alley. One ongoing topic of discussion in martial arts practice is the execution of martial arts skills *on the street.* An ever-changing standard of effectiveness has been applied to almost every style, and every technique within every style, in some magazine article or another. Comparing various martial arts to see which works better on the street has led to the extreme case of the Ultimate Fighting Challenge, in which supposed representatives of various styles duke it out in a no-holds-barred competition to prove who and what is the toughest. Most true martial artists cringe at the mention of these types of contests, because they not only bear no relationship to real martial arts and all that the training stands for, but also do not reflect the realities of the street that they advertise.

Avoiding Violence

The street confrontation has to take into account a whole range of situations, from verbal disagreements over something trivial to a planned mugging in a parking lot. In between are altercations with people who may be drunk or drugged, a conflict with a neighbor over a fence, or a domestic situation that could turn aggressive. These are self-defense situations that require some response but also clearly show the need to avoid violence. A need to prove who can win a fight will usually result in a fight that proves nothing. Martial artists prove their abilities by avoiding or defusing such possibilities. Although it is true that knowing they can back up their efforts with physical technique if required gives martial artists the confidence to try and control a situation, this subtlety seems to be lost on many who promote the fighting aspect of the martial arts. The untempered defensiveness of those who wish to know how their technique works on the street is not martial arts, not Action Kiai, but knowledge and ego out of control.

Self-Defense Training

- Remember that the principle of training is to learn new techniques and to practice them until they become second nature so that you can perform them spontaneously.

- In the learning process it is necessary to work progressively with your partner. Start slowly and with light pressure, concentrating on correctly executing the technique. As you become more advanced in your studies, you can increase the speed and power of the technique, always exercising control and caution.

- It is important to allow your partner to perform the defensive technique. It is counterproductive to resist or be stiff unless specifically instructed by the teacher. Go with the technique so that practice can occur. This will help prevent injury to yourself or your partner.

- Constantly watch for the safety release signal (three taps from the hand or foot on the body or floor, or verbal signal *matte*, stop or wait), release your partner immediately, and assist him.

- Be aware, careful, and focused when you are training any technique with a partner, and learn different responses against the same attack.

- Learn self-defense with the same intention as learning first aid; use it only in a real emergency.

- Don't apply fancy techniques. Train in simple and practical techniques until you gain expertise in that level.

- Don't underestimate your adversary.

- Don't feel shy about asking for help.

- Be diligent and persevere in your practicing; it may save your life or the life of someone you love.

- Don't abuse your power or authority; be proud of solving an extreme situation without fighting or physical action.

- Remember that the best self-defense is to have a clear mind and peaceful spirit, to enjoy life, and to share it with others.

© Claudio Iedwab

To help prevent injury during self-defense training, allow your partner to perform the defensive technique rather than resisting or stiffening up.

Exercising Restraint

Those who challenge the usefulness of martial arts training for health, fitness, and sport rather than self-defense are failing to realize that even on the street there are rules. There are serious repercussions for hurting someone, whether it is a contest, a barroom brawl, or a true self-defense situation. The legal standard of self-defense is high and difficult to prove in court. Additionally, the more you train in self-defense technique, the more responsibility you must accept for using that technique. Clearly, the greater the ability to control or deflect an opponent without having to kill him to stay alive yourself, the better the training and the more effective the martial art. There has to be an understanding of this in those who promote and teach martial arts and in those who participate in the training. Although the killing techniques of hand-to-hand combat developed in war situations (where insanity prevails and truly no rules apply) are interesting and valuable empirically, we must study them in context and not confuse them with martial arts. There is no question that there are situations in which it may not be possible to defend against a psychotic killer without a lethal response. It is also true that the best efforts to control a situation with minimum force can still accidentally result in serious harm. The human organism is vulnerable in a number of areas, and simply striking your head when falling can cause death. For these reasons and more, the martial artist will avoid fighting whenever possible.

Being within the Action Kiai always involves a measure of self-control. Again, the sense of freedom is always tempered with a restraint that protects the practitioner from injury, the training partners from harm, and the real world from illusions of self-importance or aggressive tendencies. It is important that the teacher train the mental and spiritual potential of a student along with the physical and that they discourage practicing with visions of defeating an enemy. Psychologically, the line between desire and necessity can become strained under tension. It is vital for martial artists to have control over their abilities and to be clear about the purpose of their training.

Expecting the unexpected allows us to be ready for good things to happen too. The concept that God, Buddha, or the universe will provide is one that the martial artist has learned to appreciate both in the training and everyday life. Improvising with what is at hand and, more importantly, *recognizing* what is available are fundamental skills for the resourceful martial artist. Learning how to go with the flow involves more than smooth technique and a relaxed state of mind. Every Kiai implies a union with the energy of your immediate and universal environment, and everyone understands this when they use the expression, things are going my way. We also intuitively understand when we seem to be walking under a dark cloud that something has to change. Martial artists view this in the same way as adjusting their attitude when practicing. Sometimes they need to distinguish when something is difficult because it truly *is* difficult from when something is not working because they have been approaching it the wrong way.

Often sincere students become frustrated because they have been practicing hard and don't seem to be making much progress. They sweat and push hard and devote more time than some others, but still their technique is lacking. This is usually because the students have become obsessed with their effort and are sweating too much on the outside of the forehead and not enough on the inside. It is easy to confuse the demands of the Action Kiai as being primarily physical, when in reality the challenge involves establishing the mind-set that motivates and releases the physical body to do what it has been trained to do. In this case, expecting the unexpected applies just as much to the training process as it does to preparing to deal with the outside world. Experienced martial artists will tell you that they are always surprised by what they discover as they train and that it is usually the opposite of what they thought they were setting out to learn. The Action Kiai is not isolated as a product of other Kiai; it clarifies truths, uncovers solutions, and springs surprises that should feed back into the training. The other Kiai, with lots of practice, can refine the lessons and make the new knowledge and abilities accessible on demand in the future.

Applying the Action Kiai

- Enjoy moving well.
- Make every effort, but let it happen.
- Flow with energy, commitment, and natural execution.
- When in the groove, don't force it. Don't spoil those times when things are going well by always raising the bar to test yourself to a level where frustration or failure may occur. Point yourself in the direction of excellence, and allow yourself to go there.
- Put all the elements together and just do. Don't confuse the Learning and Training Kiai with the Action Kiai. Too much analysis breeds paralysis.
- Seek the Action Kiai for inspiration and a feeling of accomplishment.
- Explore the heightened sense of awareness. Expand it to include all your activities. Look at things in new ways and with new energy. Adapt.
- Enjoy your ability and seize the day. Make each action and each moment count in a positive way.

chapter 4

The Competitive Kiai

Sparring was
originally a
method of
practice, not
one to decide
victory or
defeat.

Shigeru Egami

In North America martial arts training is most widely known for its sport aspect. When modern arts such as *karate* and *judo* were originally presented to the public after the Second World War, tournaments and demonstrations displayed the dramatic techniques and emphasized martial arts as a peaceful, sportive activity. It was a way to expose the arts to a wide audience and encourage their acceptance. It was not always easy, due to language and cultural differences, to convey the deep meanings, attitudes, and training methods of the martial arts within the context of competition.

Tournaments can be an excellent way for martial artists of different styles and levels to come together for social interaction, sharing ideas, and learning how others approach the study of the arts. Competition will benefit the development of martial artists if they can clearly see it as an application of what they are studying, and not the main purpose or content. Martial arts may contain competitive situations, but not all contests contain martial arts.

In this context, we include a discussion of the Competitive Kiai because it is so prevalent in the modern martial arts as we know them. Nonetheless, in our view tournament competition is not a necessary or required part of martial arts training and, indeed, can present some problems if not approached with good intentions and executed safely. For many, it is an enjoyable and self-improving activity that offers numerous challenges and benefits, and a focus for their practice. The opportunity to test themselves against others in a safe and healthy way, and to participate in well-organized events larger than their school and familiar group can be interesting and eye-opening. Certainly for some, this provides the incentive they need to maintain the intensity of training. It is an area in which teachers can direct students in simple applications with easy definitions.

The skills and training of the martial arts relate to more areas of life than street-oriented self-defense or a competitive tournament. Even though martial artists try to approach their whole lives as they do their training, it is important to distinguish those areas in which the techniques may be useful but do not necessarily define the martial arts. Many people apply their training to other areas of learning, teaching, and occupation. Business, education, and the fine arts have followed the strategies and philosophies that influence the martial arts, and students are always giving testimony about how their training has influenced their lives.

The sport aspect of the martial arts is one particular area where drawing some distinctions can be helpful. Although there is no question that many schools of modern martial arts have incorporated tournament competition as part of their curriculum, there are also many who have not and who believe it is not an appropriate or productive part of the training. There is considerable evidence that the founders of the modern martial arts did not want their styles turned into sports. On the other hand, many practitioners realized that tournaments and demonstrations could have a profound influence on popularizing the activity and allowing it to spread to many countries. Today we see judo and recently taekwondo accepted in Olympic level competition. This has helped legitimize and standardize the practice and promotion of these skills.

Some aspects of martial arts training lend themselves more readily to sport competition than others. Kumite or sparring has enough similarities to boxing and wrestling (which have long been accepted in Western sporting traditions) that conceiving a set of rules for scoring and judging was not too difficult. Other areas of the training, such as kata and meditation, are perhaps more important to developing the student within the art, but are difficult or impossible to bend to a sport application. Although they are not found at the Olympics, kata competitions are included at most martial arts tournaments, where divisions range from traditional kata to free-style performance set to music. These categories, which can include costumes and special effects, are

The acceptance of Taekwondo in Olympic level competition has helped to standardize and legitimize the art.

judged much like figure skating competitions and include both technical and artistic impression elements.

Keeping Competition in Perspective

As far as training the mind and body, competitive martial arts can be missing important dimensions. When viewed from the proper perspective, martial arts can include a tournament application. However, it is important that people not construe the sport alone to be true martial arts. The attitude in which one approaches the Competitive Kiai is vital to maintaining the balance of ideals and results that martial arts embody. It is also important to recognize that the martial artist should have many years of study and participation long after a competitive career has run its course.

The concept of winning a competition and defeating several opponents seems to coincide directly with the combative roots of martial arts practice. On the surface this appears to be true and is the reason so many people accept the idea of martial arts training being a sport. The philosophy, ethical standards, and health and fitness foundations of the arts are less apparent to those outside the training, however, and, unfortunately, can be overlooked. Although it is true that the traditions of loyalty and good behavior that define competing honorably closely mirror the etiquette of the martial arts, there is considerable difference between the integrity of character required to play fair and win and lose gracefully in a game or sport, and the legal and moral implications of using techniques that could injure or cause death. Tennis, basketball, and track and field are not the same as martial arts. Ideally, on a recreational level, individuals should pursue these activities for their health and social benefits. On a competitive level though, sports take on different attitudes, priorities, and content. Taken to the extreme, many of our modern TV sporting events have come to resemble big business, absurd entertainment, and even organized warfare.

Nevertheless, for some people, competition raises the level of performance. Individuals who are seeking excellence often find that participation in competition sharpens their abilities and motivates them to do better. By its nature, the process winnows out from the crowd elite athletes who are the best at what they do, according to the rules of their sport and the standards of the associations that govern them.

The Competitive Kiai heavily emphasizes improvement and maximizing potential. It can stretch the limits of previous achievement. This is the primary goal, and all other elements aim toward this result. In the martial arts, students can orient the Learning, Training, and Action Kiai toward this objective but only to the point at which the competition steps outside the regular training to focus on the art of winning.

Many competitors in all areas of sport pursue a philosophy of achieving excellence individually that they hope will create winning results. Others rely on a desire to win exclusively and use the need to beat their opponents as their primary motivation. Although this works for some (when competition unleashes extraordinary energy and fighting spirit), it can present problems for those following the Do study of martial arts. Because this training is already structured around the principle of self-improvement, it is better for students to pursue this attitude toward their involvement in competition. By directing their thoughts and energies toward competition as an *application* of their training without being consumed by the need to win, they can achieve balance, but it can be a slippery path on which the student requires constant vigilance.

Whether practicing or competing, the martial artist's focus should always be on self-improvement, not on racking up wins.

This is the key to the Competitive Kiai: work for excellence while keeping in perspective the purpose of competition and remembering the important principles of martial arts training so you do not confuse the two. The biggest danger in competition is becoming obsessed with winning. The old adage, "It doesn't matter whether you win or lose, it's how you play the game," is nowhere more important than in martial arts competition. The martial nature of the teachings and the potential for abusing these skills underscore the need to exercise caution, respect, and diligence. We must remember that there is only one champion and at best a couple of near winners. At the end of the day, the hundreds or thousands of competitors who do not find themselves among the winners must go home with something more than a losing feeling and a plastic consolation medal. Because the main purpose of martial arts training is self-improvement, the only reason to spend the time, money, and energy pursuing tournament situations is if you can learn something that benefits the martial artist inside, not just the competitor wearing a number for the day.

If martial artists can engage the attitude of the Learning Kiai, apply the work of the Training Kiai, and focus and relax so the Action Kiai can surface, they will be practicing martial arts and applying them in a competitive situation. The Competitive Kiai combines excellent performance with analysis of improvement, not for winning next time, but to make the experience meaningful and worthwhile.

Learning From Competition

By maintaining the Learning Kiai as a component of the Competitive Kiai, you will acquire knowledge and experience that you can take back to your training. If you continue to learn when you compete, you will always *win*, even if you do not place on the winners' board. To the martial artist, this is not idle compensation, but a fundamental truth of the Competitive Kiai. There are two main components to understanding the Competitive Kiai: the first is that the purpose is to improve and achieve excellent performance, and the second is that competition is an application of your martial arts training, not the training itself.

Modifying Training Techniques

With this in mind, you can modify training techniques to suit the demands and specified rules of formal competition. As we have mentioned, because most official competition rules award points for offensive scores only, students approach kumite differently in tournament than when practicing it as a defensive art. This is a concern for many martial arts teachers when their students participate in competition, because it reverses the strategic and ethical basis for the training in that type of technique. Similarly, when students perform kata for the subjective rating of a panel of judges, elements of entertainment and performance will enter the evaluation where certainly the choreographers of the traditional kata intended or implied none. With modern freestyle competition in which performers compose kata for the purpose of showing well or making an impression on the judges, they will modify technique from training purposes to what highlights their particular strengths. This can threaten the self-improvement aspect of the Competitive Kiai, for it will place little emphasis on rectifying the student's training weaknesses.

When training in the martial arts, we must get over the natural tendency to practice what we know rather than display to others the things we do not know and that require work. The rule of thumb in competition is to rely on technique that works and that you can control. It is not the time to try something new or experiment with your technique. The place for that is in the dojo with practice partners, where you can systematically analyze the advantages and disadvantages of defenses, attacks, and counterattacks and formulate a response to weaknesses.

Recognizing Skill and Weakness

If students can go to a tournament with a good attitude and a discerning eye, then theoretically they can learn much from their own performances, those of their direct opponents, and through the careful observation of other competitors, the mistakes and victories going on around them. They must be careful not to get so caught up in loyalty to the home team or dojo that they fail to recognize the abilities and strong performances of those who are competing against their friends and dojo colleagues. The current trend of cheerleading from the bleachers is improper behavior for good sports and martial artists. We should applaud excellent performances and support friends in their efforts, but it is easy to lose perspective regarding training goals, traditions, and the respectful etiquette of the dojo in tournament environments.

Balancing Practice and Competition

The Competitive Kiai is an approach to mastering the effects on the mind and body of a particular artificial set of circumstances that are stressful, unpredictable, and easily changed by emotions. The physical effects of adrenaline, fatigue, and injury take on a different tone under these conditions and can produce varied results in the body and psyche of the martial arts student. The individual, with the help of seniors and teachers, should be able to sort out what is useful and desirable from the experience with a little analysis. Students must balance participation in competition with serious practice in other areas that do not have such pressures in order to keep the training well-rounded and productive. Practice oriented only toward the tournament that weekend will shift the priorities of the student, teacher, and school away from the central Kiai of the training process and thus away from the fundamental building blocks of the martial arts.

Any positive effects from winning medals or trophies are temporary, like the wilting laurel leaves on the heads of the original Olympians. They do not produce the long-term, life-altering results that daily training provides and can leave the students feeling empty when the next champions take their places on the weekly podium. Students can spend a lot of time and resources pursuing ephemeral goals that, if invested otherwise, could bring benefits and illumination of a far more valuable nature.

Preparing for the Demands of Competition

There are many rigors associated with tournament competition other than the moments of direct competition. The preparation in the days before, nutrition, sleep, nervous anxiety, distractions, transportation, equipment, registration, and so on, will likely affect the performance more than the training in technique was able to improve it. The attitudes, training, and readiness of your opponents are out of your control, as is the quality of the judging. These elements will greatly influence achieving *results* in the tournament, but if you have approached the competition with Competitive Kiai, then your *success* will not necessarily be affected.

Learning how to control the mind and body in reaction to the demands of competition is more important to martial artists than beating their opponents. The Competitive Kiai would suggest that with good training, adequate preparation, and a Teflon-coated attitude during the day of competition, good results in the tournament will come as a consequence.

Visualizing Possible Scenarios

There are many lessons to learn in applying training in other areas, and as long as you keep these in mind, competition offers some interesting challenges. You should never confuse the trials of tournament as any approximation of a real self-defense or combat situation. Although some colors of the palette may be similar, the final painting is of a different scene altogether. Overconfidence brought on by a winning attitude can prove deadly in the wrong circumstance. One thing that competition and real combat situations do share, however, is the element of the unexpected. This is a challenge that you can meet only through advanced preparation and training.

Just as in the case of street mugging scenarios, the act of visualizing in advance what might happen in competition and how you would react to it is useful and interesting. This type of preparation is essential to rehearsing both the mental and physical processes, and provides a way of uniting these as well as connecting reality with training. Although the visualization rarely coincides with the eventual outcome, it does help the student overcome fears and be prepared for the unexpected.

Physical mimicking of potential situations, ranging from setting the environment to acting out responses is also helpful, because it engages the tactile senses directly and allows you to examine unconscious responses to light, sound, smells, and so on. Students preparing for competition seek to expand their range of sensitivity in practice to concentrate it during a tournament scenario. Clearly, the more they train in surroundings that are less than ideal and full of distractions, the more they will be able to deal with competition conditions.

Maintaining the Dojo Mind-Set

Although it is important to think ahead and imagine what tournament day might bring, it is a mistake to turn the dojo into an environment like the one at tournaments. Rather, martial artists are interested in extending the familiar environment of the dojo with them wherever they go, reminding them of their best performances when they were relaxed, centered, and moving well. This is the only center that they can realistically hope to control. If students wish to access the energy of the Action Kiai, that bubble or sphere of calm, radiant energy that surrounds them must transfer to the application of the training. This is why it is so important to have the right reasons for participating in competition in the first place and the constant feedback of self-evaluation and proper coaching to remind the student to maintain a positive and productive attitude. This is not an easy thing to do when the excitement of competition and the possibility of winning are so seductive.

For a tournament to deserve the designation of the martial arts, it should be a serious affair. At least, all participants should bow when they enter the

Students should always carry to competition the respect and quiet determination that they practice in the dojo.

hall and when they enter the ring. They must pay respect to the officials and fellow competitors with a bow and shake hands with their opponents both before and after any event. If the students can carry to the event the respect, attitude, and quiet determination of their daily practice in the dojo, then they will be participating with the Competitive Kiai of the martial artist, and their training, intensity, and focus should bring excellent results.

The fact that we rarely see these events convey the traditions and special character of the martial arts dojo indicates how far some tournaments have strayed from the path of the training. As a result, many schools that promote and emphasize competition have lost much of the original purpose, focus, and quality that the founders instilled in their respective arts. No wonder the popular media and the public have many misconceptions about the nature of martial arts training, when the public face presented conveys a distorted picture.

Dealing With Fatigue and Injury

Fatigue is natural when participating vigorously in competition. Sometimes you cause it by exerting yourself in many events and sometimes by waiting around for your turn. When fatigued, focus on accomplishing small steps that will lead to making the whole. Letting go in this moment does not mean giving up the task, but it means freeing yourself of superfluous baggage, emotionally, mentally, and physically. It will lead to your primary resources and the way you were in training. Remind yourself to return to the basics in technique, and rely on your Training and Action Kiai to back up your performance. Repeat in your mind your name, where you are, and what you are doing. Do not question your situation, because fatigue can answer more quickly than you can think or move. Fatigue will respond with a "get out" mechanism and urge you to stop suddenly. Your senses will shut down, and your confidence can break down quickly. Do not force or push yourself and produce unnecessary injuries. Rest when necessary. The competition is not more important than health and well-being. You should revere anxiety as a consequence of the fatigue. Use it as a signal that you are reaching the limits of a comfort zone, so you can stretch them in a relaxed manner. Recover the direction of your mind and body by focusing on using small muscles, such as eyelids, mouth, cheeks, or tongue. When one part of the body is fatigued and not responding, focus on relaxing other parts to restore the connection of the mind and body. You can do this by visualizing a melting block of ice or flicking water from fingers, toes, wrists, and ankles. Facilitate the breathing by relaxing jaw and neck muscles. This also helps unlock the connection between voice, emotion, and inner thoughts. Change body motions and rhythm, breathing patterns, and tactics. This breaks the patterns that cause the fatigue.

The most important thing to remember if an injury occurs is that fighting with an injury can be dangerous and potentially life threatening. Pain works as a safety mechanism to avoid serious damage, and it is relative to individuals and their circumstances. We do not advise training with any injury that can be aggravated by the performance. Training should not interfere with the healing process. However, you can manipulate minor pain into a tool to forge a beneficial result. Some minor injuries can motivate mental focus, relax unnecessarily tensed body parts, and refine mechanical control. You can override the pain sensation by focusing your attention on a major task rather than the pain. Regardless of the limitations a minor injury may cause, visualize yourself performing with excellence during the event as a continuation of your dojo practice.

Essentials of the Competitive Kiai

If you enter the arena of competition as a martial artist, there are many things to remember, many preparations to make, and many affirmations of purpose, perspective, and result that you must form and repeat throughout the experience.

Focus and Intensity

The biggest challenge when students participate in a tournament is maintaining the focus they require to perform at their best. The training beforehand has prepared their bodies and the connections with their minds. In their practice the students have engaged the Training Kiai toward developing their attention to a high level of interest without distraction. The Competitive Kiai concentrates that energy by uniting attention with intensity, progressively creating competition readiness. The focus the Competitive Kiai requires is the ability to keep the concentration available yet have the facility to switch tasks, when and where you require it.

It is possible to explain some rude and boorish behavior displayed at modern tournaments as misguided attempts to stay in the competition zone at all times rather than only when necessary. The Competitive Kiai by contrast, directs students to conserve and use energy effectively. The concept recognizes that the traditional acts of preparation and respect are the techniques by which martial artists focus the mind and tune to the physical signals and presets with which they have been practicing daily. The Competitive Kiai is the channel by which they connect with the inner calm and responsive energy they have been cultivating, to apply them to the task at hand.

Etiquette

The teachers and the school are ill serving their martial arts students, especially those in the formative years of their character, if they do not provide them with the guidance and insight that allows them to proudly display their adherence to the etiquette of martial arts engagement rather than be embarrassed by it. If their practice does not give them the skills to overcome the simple disappointment of a misplaced technique or losing a match or receiving a mistaken judgment, then what value does it have in developing character? If frustration and other emotions give way to anger and aggression in the artificial arena of competition, then dangers may lurk in the real world for the student weighed down by false expectations and mistaken priorities.

Martial artists with Competitive Kiai must remain true to their training, otherwise they should just go play tennis. There at least spectators remain quiet and do not interfere with the play, and athletes who ignore the rules and disdain the etiquette of congratulating their opponents and the judge, by tradition at least, are held in disdain. Respect for tradition and adherence to etiquette are central to the martial arts and should be in evidence at tournaments and elsewhere.

Martial artists with good training will approach any application of their knowledge, in the forum of competition, business, public speaking, teaching, technical fields, service industries, and so on, with confidence and determination. The ability to learn and improve, accept responsibility, and maintain integrity and discipline are the real skills that will set them apart. Martial arts from the strategic point of view have gained a lot of attention in business, sport psychology, and self-help formats. However, these superficial observations focus on winning alone, without looking carefully at the definitions of success and the processes of attaining it.

Trust and Confidence

People associate positive self-image and an aura of confidence with those who train in the martial arts. Most believe that this is a result of the self-defense aspect, that fearing no one naturally leads to self-assurance. Those who train are of the opinion that it has more to do with the daily progressive improvement in their ability to perform tasks and objectives that at one time seemed impossible. This trust in their training and teachers is the same mindset they must convey in the Competitive Kiai. It actually emanates from the fundamental principles of the training, and balance requires that there also be equal shares of humility and truthful self-analysis. The Learning Kiai must always bring students back to earth, to what they still need to learn and what they can reexamine. Too much emphasis on winning can have the undesirable effect of turning self-confidence into arrogance. For the majority, who do in fact lose most of these competitions, weakness and negativity can undermine the goodwill and belief in the ability to overcome obstacles that the Training Kiai has provided.

Overcoming Fears

The trust and confidence of the Competitive Kiai demand that students learn to face their fears and overcome them by dealing with them directly. Certainly competition can provide exercises in fear that would not and should not normally be found in your own dojo. We could argue that fear has no place in a martial arts tournament as well, but the reality of the competitive environment and the atmosphere that surrounds it offer plenty of opportunity for insecurities to develop into fear.

As we have seen, the primary fear is of failure. Adhering to the principles of the Competitive Kiai will sidestep a reliance on tournament results to dictate success and failure. The next most common concern, which is harder to dispense with, is the fear of getting hurt. Getting hurt can take the form of physical injury and, less visibly, psychological damage to those who are young or have not received the support and preparation necessary before participation.

We believe that many people, especially children, have discontinued their journey on the martial arts path because of negative experiences in competition situations. Many adults are reluctant to begin or resume training because of the fear of sustaining an injury in competition that could derail their physical fitness program or affect their ability to carry on their livelihood. Good training, proper equipment, and diligent and consistent judging can go a long way toward eliminating tournament injuries. Although accidents can happen (just as they do in other sports), a safe, enjoyable experience should be possible. Much depends on how the teacher prepares the student for the competitive arena and whether the participant has been forced to be there.

Staying Calm, Cool, and Collected in Competition

To combat fear and anxiety in a competitive situation, it is helpful to remember that fear is in the person not in the place. Some places, sounds, smells, and rhythms can trigger anxiety in a person. A way to avoid its effects and prevent the trigger from acting is to carry within you your positive cues that will stimulate confidence and concentration:

Smells—Gi, gym bag, personal towel with a familiar (pleasant) aroma to link you to your accustomed state of good performance.

Sounds—Kiai, breathing sounds, hands at the sides slapping the gi when bowing.

Place and rhythm—Follow your usual warm-up routine; respect courtesy and etiquette procedures; wherever you go conduct yourself as if it is your dojo.

The Competitive Kiai must be a positive experience for all concerned. Prioritize good health and happiness over results, whatever they may be. Mentally make of your competitors friendly figures, so that you do not see them as strangers. Once you are in a familiar place with people that you know who have come together to join in competition, then your performance leads toward excellence in a natural way, with the confidence expressed by playing at home. Good performances are based on good experiences.

It is not enough to speak positively to yourself; you should act, think, and feel positive. In this way your attitude is reflected in your circumstances, and you express confidence in your performance.

Creating a Positive Learning Environment

Good teachers who can convey the priorities of the Competitive Kiai and maintain strict vigilance in the dojo and the competition floor can create a positive learning environment for their students. Unfortunately, it is hard for them to control what is happening in other schools. This increases the risk and uncertainty of the tournament setting for those wishing to participate in martial arts safely. Although it is the unknown that should provide the challenges students practice to overcome, teachers must balance this benefit with the other influences and potential sabotage of the training program their students will experience.

The Competitive Kiai is a mechanism to extend the boundaries of the training method by enabling strategic objectives. It also serves as a checks and balances valve to keep things in perspective. Fair play and creative solutions that benefit all parties, whether in business, learning, or community relationships, are more important than who comes out on top.

Coaches who can motivate as they moderate the attitude, energy, and application of skills are vital to good performance. Conducting yourself with sporting behavior and respect for fellow competitors and officials is necessary and definitely part of what the game is about. For competition, we must remember, is a game. As a way of life it can lack meaning and objectivity. Although you can win many plastic trophies and even golden geese, doing so hardly matters when you distill life to the simple pleasures and realities of health and happiness. It can seem easy to evaluate yourself through the structure and imposed limits of formal competition, but because martial artists should not limit themselves by what is *easy,* more substantial parameters for success must develop out of the energy and time invested.

Negative Effects of Constant Competition

The modern world is clearly a competitive place, and we can argue that any advantage you obtain is a good thing. However, more individuals are examining the negative effects that the stress of constant competition has on their lives. The psychology of group dynamics and business behavior is bringing about changes from traditional practices in the name of productivity. We seem to be recognizing that, although companies still compete with each other fiercely for market share and survival, within each company more teamwork is necessary. Working for a collective good that recognizes individual members for their abilities and their contribution to the whole creates a better work environment, more loyalty, and less waste of time and energy. Although some corporate cultures are slow to change, service industries and educational institutions are working to provide incentives and promote the idea of working cooperatively. The same is true of martial arts environments, where many teachers and schools are reevaluating their emphasis on competition and stressing instead the health and fitness focus of their training.

Overcompetitive Attitude

When we examine Competitive Kiai, we must distinguish between what is competitive attitude and what is competition. There are many business, school, and sport applications in which the need to compete is clearly defined. There are people who thrive on competition; it provides their motivation, excitement, and reward. They are drawn toward areas that use their competitive instincts and compensate them for their skills. For some, the competitive arena completely subsumes them. They are unable to turn it off, even in areas of their lives in which it is unnecessary, inappropriate, or in some cases detrimental. Families, friendships, and communities can feel the direct or indirect effects of a competitive attitude gone wild.

The interests of martial artists engaged in competition, whether tournament or business, will turn toward the warrior strategies and philosophies the traditions embody. Although these relate to combative situations, both in individual and collective engagements of the enemy, martial arts students must recognize the limitations of their application and the need for balance through peaceful and constructive philosophies as well. Sun Tzu's *The Art of War* and Miyamoto Musashi's *The Book of Five Rings* are the two most popular historical texts of martial strategy and technique that have survived to the present day. Many business people today are following the teachings of these works, written in times of war and feudal conflict, to gain an edge in their struggles. Less well known in the business world but more useful to the martial artist in training are the philosophies of simplicity, peace, and refinement embodied in the works of Zen or Taoist masters. The strategic prowess of these masters lay in avoiding, deflecting, or subduing the attacks of their opponents and thus winning their battles by not engaging at all.

By choosing to play in a particular arena (i.e., the tournament floor or the stock trading floor), you have agreed to compete according to the rules of the game, or in some arenas, to ignore the rules. Nevertheless, all parties understand that they are engaging against each other for the goal of supremacy. If you carry this attitude into other areas of social interaction where it is not relevant or where other participants are not approaching it competitively, difficulties can occur.

As we have seen in previous discussion, there is a lot more going on in the martial arts dojo than who can beat whom in a three-minute sparring session. It is not important who can kick higher or faster than someone else. This constant comparison in a range of parameters is common among those who wish to approach their training competitively. It is a frequent result of participation in tournaments but is not confined to those situations. A competitive, or more properly, an overcompetitive manner, regardless of the origin, can wreak havoc on an individual's progress and disrupt the camaraderie and training philosophy of the school.

Measuring Yourself Against Competitors

The primary problem for students who are always measuring themselves by those around them is that it is a process and an attitude that is too exterior. By constantly relying on the performance of others to gauge their own, students are defining themselves mentally and physically in relation to others. This is contradictory to recognizing and developing the self, and it is similar to always observing your image in a mirror. Training with a mirror, figuratively or literally, means that your attention and mental visualization are always out there. The process of reacting and adjusting to what you see, the concept of self, and the circulation and expression of personal energy can become hopelessly entwined with false impressions. If such students take away the mirror or the competitors, they are often unable to perform without the feedback obtained from their comparisons. This is true of techniques, self-awareness, and mental evaluation.

Often teachers or coaches will try to break through this codependency with their insights or observations, and students will reject them because they do not match the view of themselves obtained by their comparative analysis. In the case of tournament competitors, having beaten another to win a trophy is sometimes sufficient answer to any criticism or constructive improvement a third party offers.

Strategically, students in this position have lost control of their destiny. Other people and external factors are dictating their progress. Their abilities become merely reactions to what is going on around them. To martial artists with Competitive Kiai, this is not acceptable; it contradicts what they want from their training. Defining and holding the center—mentally, physically, and spiritually—is what the study of martial arts is about.

Losing Sight of the Big Picture

Those who embrace the competitive approach are often blindly adamant about the necessity for competition and insist that it is the only way to practice martial arts. They can become frustrated with those who claim no interest in or benefit from competitive participation. Although most other sports recognize a separation of recreational and competitive levels of play, in the martial arts this separation is obscured. At times it is even confusing to those involved in the study. Those outside are rarely aware that there is anything but competition as the goal of the training, so pervasive has been the influence of tournaments, particularly in North America.

It might be useful in the discussion to remember that equipment sales and advertising revenue largely depend on the continued dominance of competition in the martial arts. Similarly, the large associations that organize the established modern martial arts systems rely on the membership fees, tournament dues, and licensing arrangements that are tied to sanctioned competition. Much political pressure has been put on individual instructors to tow the party line as far as how they organize their schools. Most associations are structured according to a hierarchy dictated by the competitive process. Certification and education focuses entirely on coaching and judging for tournaments. Teacher development and expanding the recreational participation of martial arts students receive little support. This is especially true for children in martial arts schools who must attend tournaments to change their belt level and graduate through the system. The financial incentives to a school or tournament organizer from event fees; spectator tickets; and refreshment sales to parents, grandparents, brothers, and sisters who come out to support a child competing are not to be ignored.

What happens to the balance of philosophy and application under these circumstances? We believe that too many people are being placed in competition before they have the skills, awareness, and maturity in the arts that the Competitive Kiai requires. It is important for the future health and popularity of the martial arts that we address these concerns. Modern parents are concerned about the attitudes their children acquire and are seeking holistic activities for them to participate in. The martial arts provide excellent educational opportunities for developing character, and we should not distort their true purpose.

Martial arts teachers, parents, and even students themselves have a responsibility to look seriously at the role of tournaments within the martial arts. Participation can be good for some young people and devastating for many others. The physical and psychological risks for children are high, and arguably unwarranted, given all that the martial arts can offer apart from the competitive sport aspect. Increasingly, there is debate among students and teachers about the shifts in direction that modern martial arts are taking. At elite levels there is acceptance at the Olympics and media interest in staged spectacles of fighting and wrestling, and yet at the grass roots level, more and more schools are returning to holistic traditions and the mind and body philosophies of the original founders.

We address the Competitive Kiai from the point of view of the positive elements it has to offer to the training and the aspects noncompetitive martial artists can apply to other areas of their lives where a winning attitude is needed.

Setting Goals

Students make many choices within the Competitive Kiai. To remain balanced in the martial arts training, you must decide how far down the competitive path you will stroll. It is appropriate to determine early what constitutes a peak performance and when you should achieve it. Enjoying the process of training toward the performance is important, and it is also helpful to check back with clear goals in mind when assessing your progress. The Competitive Kiai works better out of inspiration (from the inside out) than motivation (from the outside in).

Martial arts students engaged in competition will have to make choices about what they are prepared to sacrifice to achieve their goals. They must ask what aspects of their training might suffer and how they will keep a balance between the desire to win and the need to further their training. Martial artists will always play the game as good sports, regardless of the other competitors' priorities. They will become aware of those who do not recognize the rules of the game. Although making new rules may work in applying skills as an entrepreneur, inventor, or revolutionary, it is outside the definition of formal competition. This is why some martial artists find competitive goals (whether formal or informal) restrictive, not because they want to cheat or ignore the rules, but because they aren't interested in playing the game in the first place. It doesn't interest or challenge them, and in most cases the rewards are insufficient for the effort.

Competing with others or with themselves can provide martial artists with enemies they don't need, enemies they have welcomed into the training area where they practice to defeat real enemies. For many artists, it doesn't make sense. They recognize that after competition, they must transform these achievements to tools for better living, and therein lies the real trophy.

A common dead-end road that students can travel is shifting their attention away from competing with others only to become bogged down by competing with themselves. Then the enemy really has been welcomed inside the secure enclosure and is free to undermine the Competitive Kiai from within. Good is never good enough, and in an obsessive state the mind and body can end up at odds with each other. Progress becomes only linear at best and not the multidimensional lattice structure that builds strength, depth, flexibility, and character.

The Competitive Kiai implies that you will concentrate your energies in a tight focus to achieve specific goals but will also have the presence of mind and balance to keep these goals in perspective. Competing for the sake of competing is not in union with the energies that fuel martial arts training. Applying the mental techniques and the lessons of the physical manifestations of the training to areas beyond the martial arts is beneficial if done for the right reasons. Martial arts competition is not the epitome of this type of application at all, but it can be interesting and useful if you apply the feedback from it correctly during training.

We believe that the future evolution of the martial arts will be strongly influenced by the debate over what role, if any, competition plays in the training of an individual and in the life of the dojo community. We may see an increase in the trend, already present, to separate the sport from the art and the serious study of Budo.

Applying the Competitive Kiai

- Take each practice session as if it is the last before the event. Do not think that what you do not do today you will do tomorrow.
- Increase the intensity progressively.
- Do what you know and know what you do. Add creativity and spontaneity.
- Listen to your teacher or coach. Experience is a good thing only when you apply it.
- Practice gives confidence.
- If you didn't train properly, do not participate in the event. If you lose you can easily blame yourself, and if you win, a false sense of security can grow inside you. Neither result reflects the reality that you would like to build.
- Remember that fellow students and teachers may need your assistance during competition with their equipment, registration, warm-up, and so on.
- If you are observing the performance of others, do it to learn from the experience, without criticism.
- Raise your endurance to achieve a comfortable aerobic condition before your performance. Do not expect to get there during your kumite or kata; it could be too late.
- In competition, let the achievement of this state of expression be your inspiration instead of your motivation; in this way your practice is in tune with any task you approach.

chapter 5

The Meditative Kiai

The moon's
reflection on
the surface of
the stream
does not
move, does
not flow away.
Only the
water goes by.

Taisen
Deshimaru

We all meditate at one time or another. Meditation is in some ways a mental process that directs the mind inward and outward at the same time. We can often find ourselves staring off into space while our minds are elsewhere or contemplating the grain in the wood of our desks, admiring its form and line. Both are aspects of meditation, being able to detach the mind from immediate surroundings or to focus it on some intrinsic beauty near at hand. Generally, though, we think of meditation as an active mental discipline, one in which a student seeks to learn and to explore the mind and the nature of its integration with the body.

Martial artists are acutely interested in learning to control this threshold in the mind. They use the physical practice of movement to shape and refine the action of the body. The mind coordinates this. The mind is directed in a similar way by other parts or regions of the mind, and we can train it to perform through practice. Meditation is an exercise for this purpose and a way to apply these skills to pursue spiritual, mental, and physical goals.

Looking Inward by Looking Outward

The Meditative Kiai recognizes the process of examining self and awareness, but its method is detachment from its environment and surroundings. Surprisingly, we obtain this detachment by subsuming the self completely *in* its surroundings—amplifying the senses and focusing on the experience of being in that moment. This is looking inward by looking outward, a simple understanding that can be difficult to describe. The idea is that to really know yourself, you need to turn off certain processes of thinking and analysis or retune them toward experiencing. Thoughts about what you are experiencing, or what you have experienced, or what you may in the future experience are not the experience itself. By taking up more room in the mind with the full measure of the senses, you quiet these other thoughts. As an illustration, think of voices in our heads; by learning to focus on the few voices that we want to hear and understand, we can let the others pass beyond our range of listening. This is much like voices in a crowded room that we hear but do not bring into the mental listening area.

Some religions and spiritual sects use meditation as a way of examining their spiritual premises, but it is not necessary to approach meditation in a religious or esoteric way. The Meditative Kiai of the martial artist explores the simple relationships of breathing, thinking, and doing. That doesn't mean it won't raise some interesting questions as the student examines these relationships, but it does not presume to provide all the answers. Through visualization, concentration, self-awareness, observation, and analysis, the mind can release and use its energies and potential. Learning to direct this in positive ways and influence the balances within the operation of the mind is a useful goal of meditation.

Focusing on Your Breathing

In the martial arts, the kind of meditation that we study begins with a practice that seems mental, but its method is essentially physical. Sitting quietly in seiza, as usually occurs at the beginning and end of a martial arts class, seems mainly an exercise in sitting completely still. In reality, the students are holding themselves correctly and focusing their considerable mental efforts at just breathing. This requires energy that they must unite with a quiet spirit. The exercise is to learn how to play one note in the quiet. Imagine striking a bell or a drum without making another sound. Not the sound of moving to pick up a stick, the sound of the striking, nor the rattle of the hardware, just the sound of the waves pushing through the air.

Meditation begins and ends with breathing. We breathe in and we breathe out. The martial artist concentrates energy on the breathing out part of the cycle to animate it and draw from its power. With an influx of oxygen and ki in the system, an energetic exhalation helps to pump this energy around the body, making it strong, lubricating the mechanisms and joints, and fueling a sustained glide.

By beginning this way, in both class and life, as the noise piles up and distractions impose on their mental composure, students are able to remember and reimagine a calmer, quieter way of moving mentally. By also moving physically in a manner that emulates the desired state of the mind, students can more easily maintain the connective patterns. For the Meditative Kiai of the martial artist, breathing is the focus of the mental state. The conscious awareness of it will wind its way in and out of the framework as the exercise progresses through the still state of seiza and the active state of the kata.

A Meditative Kiai that places a high demand on the system will restore the balance of intake and outflow of energy with the environment. It helps mentally to think of breathing out as giving something back to your surroundings. Making the exhalation as long and smooth as possible and avoiding the urge to gasp in air is a good exercise in controlling the body by the mind. If you apply this technique when you are tired, you will think less of what you need and become more aware of and generous with what you have. This helps you to feel better and leads the way to the cyclical recovery of energy also known as obtaining a second wind.

The martial artist practices going to and through these thresholds of energy transformation within the body. The aerobic and anaerobic crossover effect reflects the changes in body chemistry and metabolic output of respiration. You can improve basic capacities and expand tolerance and redirect feelings of discomfort. The mental state that can recognize physical signals but does not overreact can maintain vital balances within the cyclical systems. When you are flying in an airplane, it is much more relaxing when you know what sounds and sensations to expect on takeoff and landing.

Students will learn visualization through the practice of imagining the flow of air in the breathing process. They will envision a circulation of energy in the body originating in the hara and feeding from the oxygen and *prana* (Sanskrit) or ki energy obtained from the surrounding environment. A major part of the exercise is to visualize the body in the mind and adjust its architecture—the spinal alignment and positioning of the head and pelvis in relation to it. One reason for this is to provide the optimum physical conditions for the exchange of air within the body. For the martial artist, further lessons about balance, equilibrium, and relaxation are valuable. Isolating particular muscles from others that must remain without tension involves a mental picture that is accurate and accessible. Visualization helps prepare the mind and body for meditation. You can also use it to apply the resources of the mind to physical or mental problems, but meditation works by emptying the mind of dominating images.

Gorindo Meditation Technique

Many schools apply different direct techniques of meditation, although the purpose and result may be the same. The process described here is how we proceed in our school; we do not presume it to be the only correct way. We present it here as an illustration, and students of other disciplines will wish to adopt their own methods. The description begins with basic technique, and when you have accomplished that comfortably with practice, you can incorporate the more advanced approaches. For some people this process can take a long time, for others, it will take less. It does not matter. With dedication and a relaxed attitude, it will come. Let it happen naturally.

Place: Begin by finding a quiet room, a place in nature, or a spot in the dojo.

Time: Meditate at the beginning and end of practice or at sunrise and sunset.

Position: You can do this technique in seiza, sitting on a chair with the back straight, or lying down.

Breathing: Throughout the following description, breathing will proceed slowly and regularly. The inhalation and exhalation occur through the nose with the mouth closed. Exhale slowly and completely without forcing the air or going to the point where the urgent need to inhale occurs. Pause briefly. Allow yourself to inhale with the abdomen expanding gently downward and outward. Again the inhalation is relaxed and not so full as to create tension or allow the chest or shoulders to rise. The inhalation should feel like a refreshing of the system, the exhalation like a release of tension. The exhalation ideally should be longer or slower than the inhalation.

The Process

1. Description of seiza position—From a standing position, lower the left knee to the floor. Keeping the spine straight, bring the right knee down so you are in the kneeling position. Form a triangular base by bringing the feet together with the insteps flat on the floor and keeping the knees two fists apart. Traditionally the left big toe rests across the right one. Tuck the buttocks under so you are sitting on your heels with the pelvis directed up and forward, ensuring the natural slight curvature of the lower spine.

Position the head on top of the spine as if suspended from a string. Imagine the nose, throat, solar plexus, and hara in one vertical line. Tuck the chin in slightly so that the ears, shoulders, and hips are in one plane.

Place your right hand palm up in the center of your lap, close to your body. Lay the left hand on top of the right with fingers overlapping, opposite, and forming parallel line. For accurate placement, ensure that the fingertips of the index and central fingers of the right hand lie directly underneath and touching the large knuckles of the index and center fingers of the left hand. Bring thumbs together lightly with only the tips of the thumbs touching, not the whole thumbprint. The Zen teachers would describe this as forming "neither mountain, nor valley."

2. Closing the eyes—Initially, and for some time, the eyes remain closed to avoid visual distraction. Much later in studying meditation you can open them slightly. Eventually, when presented with the opportunity, you can keep your eyes open in a beautiful natural environment.

Once you close your eyes, you can check your position by rocking slightly forward and backward, then moving gently left to right until, like a balance scale, you come to rest quietly, aligned and in the center.

Relax the tongue and position the tip of it up and behind the top teeth. Continue to breathe in a slow, relaxed manner and begin to focus on exhaling the air.

3. Self-examination—With each exhalation begin to scan the muscles of the face, forehead, and top and back of the head to free any tension there. Continue to expand your awareness to include the other areas of the body, from the top down and the inside out. Proceed through the neck, throat, shoulders, chest, arms,

(continued)

forearms, wrists, hands, back (upper, middle, and lower), abdomen, groin, buttocks, thighs, knees, calves, ankles, feet, and toes.

Feel the skin over your whole body free of tension and refreshed. Then visualize the internal organs of the abdomen released of tension. By this time you will be aware of the beating of the heart and the pumping of the cardiovascular system forming a pulse through the body that sends nutrients to every cell.

See your lungs filling with oxygen that also fills every cell. Exhale calmly and slowly, allowing the pathways of the nervous system to share in the calming effect.

Once this harmonization of the whole system has occurred, your consciousness can expand beyond yourself and your physical container in a peaceful, universal experience.

When you wish to resume activity, take three deep breaths, slowly raise your hands in front of you, palms up, and stretch them in a large circle to the outside, returning to the abdomen. Open your eyes, bend forward, and place your hands on the floor. Raise the hips slowly, then put your toes and balls of the feet on the ground, gently shifting the weight to your feet. Flex toes, ankles, and knees, bringing your hands back close to your knees. Opening your feet shoulder-width apart, slowly straighten your legs, unroll your spinal vertebra, and resume a standing position, raising the head and finally the eyes. It is most important to not stand too quickly because loss of balance could easily result.

Advanced Methods

Once students can accomplish the preceding process effortlessly through time and practice, they can move to a level at which the awareness will focus on the breathing.

Visualize a balloon being filled with air expanding outward from the abdomen as you inhale. Empty the balloon by exhaling in double the length of time it took to inhale. With each breath increase the size of the balloon outward to include the hips and eventually the knees. The concentric circle expands like a tide or wave.

If you wish to harmonize your mind to prepare and energize your body, inhale for four counts through the nose. Imagine a path through the forehead, head, back of the head, and down the spine, hips, pelvis, lower abdomen, down to the hara. Next, exhale for six counts (later eight counts), up from the solar plexus, sternum, throat, and through the nose. At advanced levels there will be a retention or pausing of the inhalation and exhalation.

If you wish to harmonize your body to clear and energize your mind, inhale for four counts, through the nose, down the front of the body, to the hara. Exhale for six counts (later eight counts), through the spine, up to the head and nose. Here also the advanced level of practice involves a pause within the pattern.

In general, relax and let the mind be calm. Although it is empty of distraction, thoughts and awareness will pass through quietly and without disturbance. Absorb the environment and let yourself be absorbed by it. Be one in an expanded way by fusing with the elements and going back to basics. The energy that binds them together, ki, is in you too, and you also are in it. If at any point you are interrupted in the process, relax and begin again to reach the point where you left off.

© Claudio Iedwab

Relax and let yourself be absorbed by the environment during meditation.

Reaching a Meditative State

Other methods of meditation train the mind by concentrating energy and thought on something in particular, an image of light, for example, or a recited series of words (a *mantra*). In some cases, a sound is hummed, creating a vibration that is personal or with which others can join. This can give the practitioner a physical manifestation that provides a reference grid for the mental processes at the threshold of the mind and body relationship. Martial artists, however, have available a full range of physical connections in their study of meditation and need to have a calm, empty mind state. To meet the challenges embodied in the practice of martial arts, meditation provides a way to train physically without distraction, not by blocking the senses or thought processes but by allowing them to flow through, over, and around the focus of the mind. The martial artist doesn't train to improve the meditation, he meditates to improve the martial arts. This improvement benefits all aspects of life—working, sleeping, even laughing and having fun.

Concentration

Concentrating the mind on the task at hand is essential for the Meditative Kiai. We think of the word meditative as a passive description, but we must understand its dynamic qualities as well. The success of the meditative state hangs on the delicate balance between letting what happens in the mind happen and controlling the presence or absence of thought. Some have described it as "controlling the mind to let it happen." The important thing is that the Meditative Kiai has a positive energy moving forward or outward from the self at the same time it absorbs energy from the environment. Concentration works by eliminating distraction or nonessential information from the mind and the body and generating a particular wave to fill the void. Martial artists might be focusing all their power in their fingertips for a strike, for example or, contracting the abdominal muscles to absorb a blow, or gathering all their resources to leap into the air. They may need to concentrate to sustain their flow of energy over a series of moves or to endure a significant pressure for a long time. They may need to focus on keeping a line straight or a circle round (as described with their bodies or swords).

Meditative Kiai operates by finding a zone in which concentration can occur. Some teachers believe that the more you bring this to the forefront and study it, the more aware and available the technique is to the mind. Others believe that too much analysis or verbalization only clouds the issue with conscious thought, which can be subject to misinterpretation. Trying not to think is difficult, as is trying to not think of something in particular, like the aforementioned purple elephant. Powers of relaxed concentration, having confronted this as an exercise, are strengthened and become able to accomplish the task of specific application.

Self-Awareness

By taking the time to examine the workings of the mind through meditation we can reveal a great deal about the self. This is not searching to uncover deep secrets but to discover patterns that have shaped how we think. By understanding these workings in the same manner that we observe how our body reacts and learns, we can make adjustments and improvements that benefit our abilities and our happiness. We tend to avoid and be more judgmental about our mental attributes or weaknesses than our physical ones. In Western society we rarely reflect on developing the mind (or spirit) as we do the body, and we are less willing to work toward its improvement.

Many people are unaware that numerous aspects of our mental processes are not fixed as inherent characteristics or complex phenomena, but are simple skills that we can identify and practice. Their usefulness in controlling stress is one application that should encourage more people to examine how they think, in addition to what they think.

The self-awareness the Meditative Kiai induces calls for a willingness to open up and an objective, relaxed attitude about what might be revealed. Its purpose is not to define our character or lay blame for weaknesses in it, but to improve and strengthen our abilities through practice. Allowing ourselves to project a positive future while building on an understanding of the framework of the past is important. With awareness comes a choice about what information is useful to carry and what is not. The study of meditation requires some analysis over time, but the analysis is not the practice itself. Observation and contemplation are useful elements, but their value remains largely in the experience itself, not in the reflections or reverberations the experience creates.

Traditional Practices

The traditional teaching practices of the philosophies that employ meditation, such as Zen, require a dialogue with a mentor or advisor in which you can exchange thoughts and questions. This aids in self-examination by imparting an exterior point of view and helps students verbalize or visualize the process in which they are participating. Because we rarely reach answers through deductive reasoning, many illustrations and stories have developed within the traditions to position the mind and allow for intuitive comprehension of the concepts. Some have been formalized into *koan*—little poems or question-and-answer tales—that challenge the mind or illustrate concepts for a better understanding. Examples such as, "What is the sound of one hand clapping? If a tree falls in the forest does anybody hear?" are the ones most Westerners have heard in relation to Zen. There are, of course, many more.

To some people it doesn't matter whether anyone can hear a tree falling in the forest. For teachers and serious students it hardly matters whether you are in the forest at all, especially if you are so arrogant to think that if *you* are not there, no one else, including the birds and the bees can hear it. Sometimes koan challenge our abilities to understand and sometimes they just confront our preconceived notions. Self-knowledge can come from shaking things up a bit and reorganizing the chips as they fall.

The patience to ponder these riddles is a skill acquired through meditation and contemplation. It is part of the reason for the apparent obscurity of many teachings related to meditation or the philosophies of Zen or Taoism. Students are challenged to examine their assumptions and not be too quick to reject an idea because of how it first appears or what it may reveal on the surface. They learn not to be frustrated by problems that seem complex when sometimes simple truths can solve it. Martial artists are interested in these approaches because of the historical underpinnings of the activity they are involved in and because there are lessons and exercises that are immediately applicable to their training. Teachers who can impart to their students the mental and spiritual frameworks for the physical practice are valuable. Both the teacher and the student require a certain amount of patience and willingness to hear and see with an open mind.

Preparing to Walk Alone

Much of martial arts training is a gradual process of improvement. Every so often though, insights occur that can change the speed of learning or the improvement of sets of skills. Sometimes these are physical breakthroughs,

© Roxanne Standefer

Instructors help prepare students so that one day they can walk the journey alone.

such as finally achieving a level of strength, flexibility, or stamina that permits you to perform a technique more effectively. More often it is unlocking a key concept in the physics of a movement or the mental connection to a physical task that permits you to incorporate a new skill into the body of knowledge. These are psychological aspects of the process of learning that you cannot leave to the methodology of the teacher alone. The Meditative Kiai of martial artists demands that students take some responsibility for their own learning. The balance of responsibility shifts away from the teacher as the student progresses through the program. At advanced levels the quantity of the teacher's intervention gives way to the quality of the intervention.

So, although beginners are led by the hand (and sometimes the nose), both in the physical techniques and simple mental aphorisms that might accompany them, advanced students are left to walk by themselves. Teachers and senior students will make the occasional course correction, but their main work has been to prepare the path for the student to follow. Setting them on the course, cautioning them to lift their feet as they walk so they don't trip, and reminding them from time to time to stop and look around, rather than keeping their noses to the ground, prepares students for the journey they must make alone. Occasionally the teacher must let the student stumble.

Advantages of the Meditative Kiai

The teacher or school is not going to dictate the personality or character that the student must have. Although certain elements of character and integrity are required, especially by those involved in advanced levels of learning, the martial artists themselves must decide who they are and who they wish to be. Meditation alone will not make perfect people. Martial arts study as a whole does not make perfect people, but it *can* make better people.

Building Character

Character building is a goal of the training, and students achieve it through the interaction of several methods of self-improvement. The tests, challenges, and affirmations that are built into the process help students learn more about themselves, how they operate, and how they can get better at something. Knowing how you respond to small difficulties can help shape a framework for responding that you can use when the big ones come.

Weathering Storms

The Meditative Kiai helps martial artists get in touch with their fundamental spirit. The secret lies not in meditation alone, but consists additionally of the preparations for and applications of meditation in the training and in other areas of daily life. Martial artists learn that they must not be afraid of discovering weaknesses. Weak areas can then be shorn up, reinforced, or torn down and replaced by stronger, more positive characteristics. Being able to accept themselves and find a place of comfortable solitude within helps martial artists weather many storms. Advanced students have fewer illusions about being invincible, and when confronted by their insufficiency in meeting a challenge, they work to ensure that it does not happen again. Nevertheless, they continue to stand up when they fall down, even if it is the hundredth time they have been knocked over. When students can see the similarities between the roadblocks in their lives and those they encounter in their training, they are beginning to understand the Do and how to put the practice to good use beyond exercise and conditioning.

Stimulating Creativity

The fundamental spirit in all of us is an energy that has to do with what is right about us, not what is wrong or missing. Learning to touch this, to let it grow, and to express it is one joy of martial art training. Assessing what makes us have fun, inspires us, and bowls us over when we are supremely happy is more important than analyzing why we are not. In the same way that martial artists clean their minds by energizing their bodies, individuals can reanimate their characters by reaching for positive action and creativity. Building new experiences, reactions, and reasoning fills the mind so there is less room for distractions and baggage. Your energy is not confined or drained, and the more it flows or circulates, the more powerful its force.

The samurai warriors practiced meditation and the creative arts of writing and painting to calm and focus their thoughts and to fully appreciate the beauty in the art. Their aim was to take from those activities an energy and worthiness that would help them control their fears in the face of conflict.

Creativity feeds from a similar energy that is both outward and inward. Artists, writers, and inventors take in information from their environments, mull it about, then do something with it. They often need to separate themselves for a time to eliminate distractions and focus their creative energies. Although most of us have thoughts that we obtain from contemplating the world around us, few of us use those ideas to produce something new, original, or valuable. The creative process is more than just feeling creative, it is *being* creative. The Meditative Kiai stimulates creativity by clarifying thinking and providing mechanisms for directing the mind.

Most martial artists are inspired and invigorated by their training. They find they do better at school, at work, and in artistic pursuits. Some of this comes from getting exercise and being healthier, but most people who have been fortunate enough to train with a good teacher for a length of time notice profound changes in their lives. How they think, how they feel, and how they do things can be quite different from when they started. This is the result of cultivating ki energy and uniting it with mental and physical demands.

It is important to understand that martial artists do not meditate only when sitting at rest. Kihon and kata can become meditation and are exercises of the Meditative Kiai. Even though these aspects of the training are repetitive, they feel creative because of the need to treat each technique or combination as something fresh and original each time you perform it. Although actors may have played the same roles in a play each night for many weeks or months, their goal is to make the experience real and profound every time. If you are

© Melanie Lord

Kata can be considered an active form of meditation.

in the audience, you want that, too. You have come to participate in the full expression of the creativity of the writer, director, actors, and crew.

Zen Philosophy

One important lesson of Zen is loyalty to the moment you are in and the unique quality of that experience. Zen Buddhism is a religion that many people around the world practice, although it has East Asian origins. Originally known as *Chan* in China, it is thought to have been established by a monk named Boddidharma who traveled there from India. He is also credited with teaching the Shaolin monks techniques for unarmed self-defense and health improvement along with their lessons in religion and philosophy. The work of Boddidharma is commonly seen as one of the cornerstones of the martial arts.

We can separate Zen from its religious aspects of devotion, community, or positioning the Buddha as a god. Some argue that attaching Zen philosophy to a religious movement contradicts the philosophy. Nevertheless, although it is beyond the scope of this book to explain Zen at length, it is appropriate to examine briefly its relevance to the Meditative Kiai and the martial arts.

What is Zen, anyway? As a philosophy rather than a way of life, it has to do with intuitive realizations and glimpses of profound understanding. However, a great deal of discourse and writing has gone into the study of Zen around the world. We have explained much of the Meditative Kiai in terms pertaining to Zen and how we study it, especially in relation to meditation. In many martial arts schools, particularly those of Japan, many teaching methodologies and traditions also derive from Zen schools. Certainly the relation of teacher to student and the method of transmitting knowledge have similarities, but Zen attitudes, states of mind, and applications of what is learned are also central to many martial arts approaches.

There are several key phrases that are popularly associated with Zen. They have become well known, not only because of their deep meaning but also because they are accessible doors into the simple wisdom of Zen. The philosophy does not easily lend itself to preaching or proselytizing its fundamentals, because it is not Zenlike to force things to be as they should be. Zen teachings are more concerned with understanding the truths of things as they are and having clarity rather than confusion or illusion.

We can joke about being one with the universe only because we so rarely are. To contemplate the infinity of our subatomic structure (or chaos) at the same time as the subtleties of the expansion of outer space is a challenge. To do so while dealing with the immediate crisis of ensuring that we can take our next breath is a tall order. It certainly puts things in perspective.

Becoming too attached to thoughts, memories, material things, and self-impressions can lead to disappointment. At the least, it can cause discomfort in your enlightenment. Even those who have chosen to become monks and study Zen seriously acknowledge that to have a flash of clarity about something does not necessarily mean that it is easy or even possible to sustain that level of understanding or practice all the time. With work you can certainly improve, but focusing too intently on it, as on the light of a star in the night sky, makes it disappear. This elusiveness in Zen is part of the joy of its simplicity. For Zen to have a dogma about itself negates the usefulness of the teaching about letting go and going with the flow.

The martial artist has to be careful to study and understand the nature of the attachment and detachment of the mind, to and from the body, and to and from its surroundings. Too much detachment could be dangerous. Yet as we've seen, the student practices to become immersed in the body movement but able to let the body carry on while the mind is unaffected. This mechanism may be protective in the event of injury or anxiety, but it is fundamentally about choice, self-control, and prioritizing.

Accepting Simple Truths

Zen makes considerable effort to insist on simple lines, clean technique, and essential beauty when expressing ideas in movement, art, or design. This is to make clear the organic nature of what you are examining so you can understand it. To teach in this way, you begin with basic concepts and grow from there. The truth of Zen, however, is that if you honestly perceive these simple truths and integrate them into your knowledge and experience, there is no need to complete the full circle of trial, examination, example, and elimination only to come back to the beginning. In the end, the simple truths are the simple truths. Nevertheless, we feel compelled to prove to ourselves that this is so; in the West we prefer complicated explanations when we seek to understand something.

Many students expect more; they want to know the secrets and they want to know them *now!* When senior students (and those who have stayed on the path to become teachers) try to answer their questions honestly, the answers seem simplistic. Yet the impatient student finds them mysterious. The hidden meaning reveals itself to be that there *is* no hidden meaning. Enlightened martial artists who face this realize that they should just go back and train. For them the training *is* the meaning, but what they have learned is how to approach it, embrace it, and appreciate it all the more. In this way the student is advised to do by not doing, or take action by not acting.

In the case of meditation, who else can know what is going on in your mind? In physical technique, another can see that you have struck a blow or placed a kick in just the right way, and there is some evidence of its power. In seiza meditation, it is possible to observe the respiration rate, and measure oxygen content and brain waves with the right equipment, but it is still impossible (fortunately) to hear others' thoughts and view their mental images. We can demonstrate control of the physical self and others can thus infer mental control of the body. However, the mind and how it finds itself in the body is a personal experience. Through questioning, the teacher can help students reveal what processes they are going through, but language, ego, and presumption can color or cloud communication on this subject. It is probable that students of meditation cannot be sure themselves what is happening, but there is no doubt that the act of trying to find out raises some interesting questions and provides insights that can lead to understanding.

Calm, Detached State of Mind

One traditional illustration for meditation and martial arts directs students to have "a mind like the reflection of the moon upon the water." This is a concept that indicates a calm state that exists because of the moon's light and the properties of the water that cause it to reflect, but it is neither of the moon or of the water. Wind or current may cause fluctuations in the surface, yet the light is still there, though its perception is possibly fractured; certainly the disturbance does not affect the moon much or even the water. Moreover, the moon is merely reflecting the sun's light, and the wind is caused by invisible motion of waves of molecules moving from areas of high concentration to low. This movement of air can also cause clouds to form that can pass in front of the moon and obscure its light. However, the moon and the sun, for now, are still there, and the student must calm the mind and let thoughts pass through its surfaces like a gentle breeze that ruffles the leaves then settles down to let silence return. The student must have patience and restraint; the process of meditation is like that in which particles of sand eventually find their way by force of gravity, leaving the water clear. The Meditative Kiai unites this calm state with a positive kinetic energy that allows the water to flow, but flow cleanly.

Martial artists seek a state of detached mind, or more accurately *no* mind, or mushin, in which they feel connected to something fundamental, yet relaxed about not doing anything except being. People sometimes interpret this to be a mind in which absolutely nothing is going on—it is shut off. It is more accurately a mind state that cannot be distracted or affected negatively. The Meditative Kiai lets go of past performance, mistakes, or attitudes in the quest of the moment, in which the future has unfettered possibility.

Images That Promote a Meditative State

You may use the following images in meditation to promote an advanced meditative state.

- Earth—sitting on a sphere that reduces in size, disappears; you remain floating in space expanding your ki consciousness.
- Vase of water turbulent with silt (thoughts, disturbances, distractions, etc.); becoming quiet, clear, transparent, reflective, and open; experiencing gratification and comfort.
- Self as a leaf, floating on the lake, moving with the water and wind (motion meditation for kata, kumite, etc.).
- Sphere of golden light in the hara—expand.
- Sphere of golden light in the solar plexus—expand.
- Sphere of golden light in the forehead—expand.
- Sphere of golden light in the hara, moving to the solar plexus, the forehead, back to the solar plexus. Expand with a sense of love, letting go tensions and free of ties, with an inner comfort and sense of spiritual well-being (as in kata and kumite).

Loyalty to the Moment

Being in the moment does not imply that you have to stay there. You couldn't even if you wanted to. This is the simple error that most students make when trying to achieve a *satori*, or enlightening experience. When we come close to such an experience or are in fact in its grip, we try so hard to hold on, make it last, or even worse, drag it back into our mundane existence. Enlightenment is not a prize to lock up or put on display. It is a transitive experience that leaves us with a sense of having understood something important and yet, as when we awake from a dream, we cannot remember it exactly. This is a typical reaction but not a useful one if we do not choose to go there again. "Satori? Oh, yes. I've had one. Been there, done that, thanks. Next."

The Meditative Kiai accepts that we are in motion. It should be a dynamic point of balance around which nothing is still but in which there is movement correcting toward the center. The Meditative Kiai is like a fine crystal with many facets that are revealed when it is cut along certain lines. When this diamond is turned in the light, it can reflect blindingly or allow us to see colors and beauty deep inside the stone. Not all facets are shaped the same, nor is the stone necessarily symmetrical. Like a diamond, we can use the Meditative Kiai to cut the hardest materials, but it can easily be shattered by the light tap of a hammer.

Lessons From Nature

There are many lessons we can take from nature to illustrate the Meditative Kiai. It is not coincidence that those who are interested in Zen or meditation find themselves drawn to natural surroundings and seek peace and quiet in the wilderness. It is not only because they wish to eliminate distractions. For some, it is because they find that when they are immersed in nature, there is almost no need to meditate! It might be better said that the contemplation of nature and the breathing of fresh air allows the meditation to become more full, alive, and aware. In a city, or a situation that has tension, anxiety, or

© Roxanne Standefer

Immersing yourself in nature can help enhance the meditative experience.

danger, the need to meditate formally (in the conventional sense of closed eyes and quiet sitting) is more immediate and essential as a balance to external forces. Imagining a calm place in nature helps the practitioner return to relaxed clarity more readily. A period of meditation can help restore energy and cushion the blows of any external onslaught. Ideally, the more experienced practitioner can remain in a state of meditative calm longer or at least return to peaceful equanimity easily.

Embracing the Environment

It is important that students not use the Meditative Kiai to block the senses or the quality of human experience. As beings with a place in nature, it is vital that we embrace the natural environment wholly and respect its cycles and interdependencies. We are blind to essential reality if we fight this truth, and on a practical level, we are damaging our own nests.

Our human organism is a product of natural processes. We would be remiss if we were to ignore the conditioning and instincts that are simple responses to stimuli. Although some of our responses are dictated by genetics and environment, we, like many organisms, also have the ability to make choices. The fact that humans by and large haven't made good choices is probably the reason we need martial arts at all. They evolved out of our inability to make equitable arrangements to share resources and territory, and our need to defend our means of survival from others. It may be a sorry beginning for a system that has progressed into something useful and beautiful, yet as the arts continue to evolve, they can become more practical for a peaceful existence. Perhaps self-defense of the individual will give way to defense of the species and the planet.

Understanding our physical organism and exploring the mental energies that keep it going can help us improve the quality of our existence. The mind is curious by nature, yet we easily become conditioned by constant external stimuli. It takes more effort to stop the controlling effects of conditioning than to change our responses. By doing this through meditation, we gain access to tools that can break dependency and help us achieve inner freedom. Not unlike hypnotism, meditation can be used to remold patterns of behavior, emotions, and feelings. Meditation can open channels to transform personality structures and expression, but it can be easily sabotaged because it is subject to manipulation. Meditation is not an escape from reality; it is full awareness and enjoyment of the present and your presence within it.

A harmonic existence with clear mind, transparent spirit, and a conscious body is the status quo of the Meditative Kiai. Once the self has achieved a nondistracted state, it is time to expand the sphere of awareness, consciousness, and oneness with the environment. Joy and crispness of reality can provide an appreciation of life and a concrete and palatable sense of existence. Temporality and permanence fuse in a transcendental way. The Meditative Kiai will come to permeate all the other Kiai through the course of training. Its path is not linear but circular with an ever-expanding radius, like the outward reverberations of a pebble dropped in a still pool.

To go with the flow does not mean to stop swimming and drift aimlessly. A canoeist negotiating a series of rapids learns to avoid working against the current when it is flowing too strongly or when she reaches a point in the river where doing so could send her over onto the rocks. However, the canoeist knows to stay close enough to the natural flow of the stream to use its power and energy to spin off in a new direction or exit the current into an eddy. This is the same with martial arts. Increasing our sensitivity and aware-ness of the energy that flows around us is a fundamental purpose of the Meditative Kiai.

Welcoming Silence

Our verbal skills and visual sense tend to dominate our mental processes. Sitting without speaking for a while helps to stimulate our hearing, aware-ness of gravity, and tactile responses. Many people are not comfortable with silence. For some the universe becomes frighteningly loud. Some don't like to hear their own thoughts. When we look at how rarely an urban or home environment anywhere is without voices or sounds of some sort—TV, radio, appliances, trucks on the street, and so on—we realize it is a good idea to get our thoughts in order every once in a while. Silence is necessary to calm the mind before doing mental housecleaning. Meditation is one way to clean house, and exercising or working in a focused way is another. To create a craft or work of art is an enjoyable way of achieving a calm state of mind. The Meditative Kiai applies to all of these activities.

As with any exercise, practice of mind and body responses will make each step more fluid and spontaneous over time. The patience of the Learning Kiai is always useful here as is as a philosophical attitude that does not expect too much to be revealed at once. The Meditative Kiai keeps it simple. Breathe well, keep the mind clear, and move with directness. Inner transparency allows the uncovering of potential mental and physical aptitudes that we should integrate with the other Kiai.

In the same way that lifting weights at home produces a result that we can apply when we travel and carry a heavy suitcase, we can apply meditation later to any situation, time, place, and circumstance. The Meditative Kiai begins simply; when it has acquired form it grows, changes, and matures. It eventually becomes a personal expression that we can state simply as breathe, relax, smile.

There is an expression in Japanese for the inner harmony of a being. The word *wa* (harmony), in its sound and character, bears an echo that moves outward in the same way that a verbal Kiai from a martial artist emanates from the hara and expands. The Meditative Kiai helps to monitor and regulate the fine balance of the wa. The effect for the martial artist is the ability to move though the world like a camera suspended in a steadicam gyroscope. Despite being jostled around or moved up and down, the instrument renders an image that is smooth and wavelike in motion.

Keeping it simple yet treating meditation with respect will improve the mental, physical, and spiritual well being of the individual. Emulating the calm mind state achieved when sitting quietly and applying that state to other activities can be beneficial. Doing so improves productivity, reduces stress, frees creativity, and reenergizes the body. For the martial artist the Meditative Kiai is the Kiai of balance.

Applying the Meditative Kiai

- Take time to enjoy the moments you are experiencing.
  "Life is what happens to you while you're busy making other plans."
    —John Lennon

- Rely on your breathing and harmonizing the internal with the external. Be aware of body processes, sensations, and feelings. Look for similar patterns and reactions in the natural world. Emulate the relaxation and energy of nature.

- Practice meditation to clear the mind and rejuvenate the spirit. Do not carry expectations or goals into your practice. Let it happen.

- Investigate other ways of thinking and cultures different from your own. They may offer fresh insights and directions for your life. Embrace nyuanshin. Allow yourself to examine your preconceived notions, and do not be afraid to shake things up a bit from time to time.

- Recognize that you are largely responsible for how you perceive any situation and that often it is only your attitude that separates you from change or improvement.

- The world can be a noisy, busy place. Turn the volume down occasionally.
  "Remember what peace there may be in silence."
    —Desiderata

- Seek harmony.

chapter 6

The Masters Kiai

A monk asked Ryuge, "What did old Masters attain when they entered the ultimate stage?" "They were like burglars sneaking into a vacant house," Ryuge replied.

Zen Koan

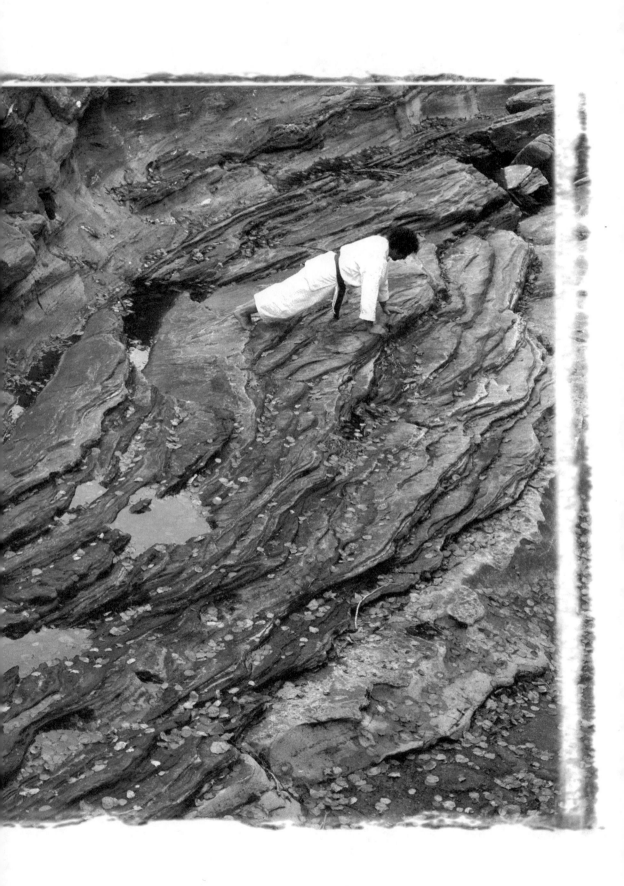

At the least, being a master in the martial arts means knowing what mastery is, even if you are unable to completely or consistently attain that state. One irony of the Masters Kiai is having a clear view of your limitations, weaknesses, and errors even though you have developed your excellence and ability to a high level.

In the martial arts, we consider perfection unattainable, in the same way that we cannot surround something of infinite size. It is just beyond reach for several good reasons, not the least of which is the arrogance of spirit required to define or proclaim it. As a goal to work toward, perfection can provide motivation or inspiration, but the achievment of perfection leaves little room to maneuver. Masters who do something perfectly always harbor the doubt (and the hope) that with another effort perhaps they could do it a little better.

Nonetheless, the Masters Kiai does not operate under false pretenses of humility about abilities or level of understanding. It is important to maintain a humble attitude, but that should come from the healthy dose of Learning Kiai or nyuanshin that the master retains. Without nyvanshin, there is no mastery by any definition.

The Masters Kiai requires integrating all the training elements. Martial artists should be confident enough of their skills and reactions to trust their ability to deal with any situation. Certainly part of what works in a self-defense scenario is conveying that confidence in a way that discourages an attack. Knowing full well what you can do and what you can't do affects strategies and choices. You should combine an awareness of your limitations with faith in the kind of magic that can occur when your survival is at stake or when you take a risk that turns out well.

Advancing Toward Mastery

Martial artists at advanced levels approach mastery of the subject as a succession of plateaus where they must take time to study the lessons of that level and reexamine if necessary what they have learned before. Although they are always ready to learn more, masters are less concerned with how many techniques they have acquired and more interested in their relationships and how to link them into a smooth, seamless form. The practice will be specific to finely tune the responses and subtle nuances of a technique, but the analysis of that practice will relate to movement as a whole and how the organism reacts to its environments.

Creating balance is a goal of any martial artist at any level. The Masters Kiai contains an energy that is capable of rebalancing and restoring the self to center. Knowing that they can return readily enables martial artists to move farther from the center. It is not fair to expect masters to never reach out to test themselves, take risks, or even fall from time to time, when they have already achieved such a high level of excellence. Experts who only practice what they know do not grow; eventually they stagnate. The Masters Kiai demands that martial artists guard with vigilance the freedom to train and improve by making and correcting mistakes. They must not allow expectations about rank and teaching qualifications to dictate the process of self-improvement, particularly when they have already dedicated so much time and effort to it.

Analyzing and Evaluating Progress

The Masters Kiai is not confined to those becoming expert at the skills they are practicing. Analysis and evaluation are necessary at all stages in the progression of learning. It is important to separate what we know and what is correct from what needs work. Students who study hard, especially those with a good teacher, can often learn a great deal early in their training. Even though they might not be able to perform consistently, they may achieve insights and capabilities beyond their perceived or expected level. In a good program, the teacher can help such students bring a balance to their training and progress in a well-rounded manner. Proper guidance on the plateau enables the route to the next level on the summit to be revealed. If the path there is too direct, neither teacher nor student will have acquired enough familiarity or knowledge about the surrounding area. As a guide or teacher, you will not be that helpful to those you may lead there; if they stumble or detour, you are both in a new territory.

Sharing Your Knowledge

Being able to share and teach what you have learned is an essential quality of Masters Kiai. Experts may be quite accomplished, but if they are unable to or uninterested in passing it on, their mastery may be illusory. You can learn a great deal by teaching another. The learning comes not so much in teaching what you know as in observing and directing a unique learning process. Even for students with the same system and the benefit of the same teacher's advice in avoiding pitfalls, each individual's path up the mountain is different. By adding the experiences of others to your own, the value of the

One of the best ways to learn is through teaching others.

experiences becomes richer. Previous answers acquire new meaning, questions get answered, and new questions get asked. Teachers learn a lot more about what they don't know. Most people who are honest with themselves as they approach an advanced level in any pursuit feel that they know less about their subject than they did before. This is only because proportionately there appears to be so much that they have yet to learn.

For the martial artist with Masters Kiai, this is a good thing. This is what keeps the learning fresh and invigorating even after many years of study. It is immensely enjoyable to learn new material or see in a new way, and it keeps the spirit, mind, and body young.

Making a Commitment

As students age they are able to employ other resources to balance those that are held in reserve. Working on the energy of mastery involves responsibility for maintaining a high degree of physical ability and mental focus in order to continue moving forward, rather than hanging onto previous victories. Masters acknowledge that there are slips and recoveries along the way, but they continue to make a commitment to sustained effort. The purpose of attaining a high level of excellence is to enjoy the benefits of being able to function well and attempt the things that require adequate preparation.

The Masters Kiai acknowledges that it is easier to sustain forward momentum than to build it from scratch. Nevertheless, masters should never be afraid to reevaluate their direction or to tear down whole sections of what they have done in order to build a firmer foundation. The confidence to begin again comes from knowing what they can do and how long it might take them to do it. The purpose arises out of interest in what is good and the knowledge that what is different may be better.

One reward of Masters Kiai is appreciating excellence and beauty. Having the opportunity to create or contribute to the excellence and beauty in the world as a result of your training is deeply satisfying. Too much humility or self-deprecation can lead to frustrating these creative energies; then they benefit no one. It is not an effective use of your training or that of the teachers and fellow students who helped along the way. For the masters, there will always be more to learn and correct, but they are philosophically resigned to allow things to be as they should be. However, this does not mean that they forsake their part in making them happen.

Thus, the Masters Kiai is similar to and intimately connected with the Learning Kiai. Rather than having the perspective of the white belt, unknowing and looking outward, the master is looking inward, knowing much but still possessing great learning potential. One analogy we commonly use in the martial arts is the story of the black belt who has climbed the mountain only to see in the surrounding vista numerous other peaks he can climb, some of which have an even higher vantage than the one he clings to.

The greatest challenge for advanced students of the martial arts is retaining their Learning Kiai, remembering the freshness and exuberance with which they approached their training as a beginner. Many who become fixated on the specific goals of the belt rank or on tournament placement become lost when they reach a level where the belt doesn't change color anymore. For those who have celebrated nyuanshin along the way, it is less difficult. They find joy in the smallest improvements and the infinite new connections they discover among the skills they have practiced for some time.

Achieving Harmony

There must be some purpose to which we can apply all this effort to integrate mind, body, and spirit. As we have discussed, the main objective of all the Kiai is to bring us into a harmony with ourselves and our environment. This can enable the masters to do great things or, conversely, stop doing things that may be in contradiction with their spirit. Many people realize that they haven't been doing what they want with their lives at all. This can happen even though they may have achieved or surpassed the goals that were set for them or that they set for themselves. This may be a result of boredom or having denied themselves options because of family responsibilities, circumstances, or lack of courage. Some people, although they do not find themselves where they expected to be, look around at where they are and discover that in fact they like it. They just may have been looking down the road rather than smelling the lilacs along the way.

Continuing to Learn

The Masters Kiai implies having a perspective on your accomplishments and realizing what improvements training in the martial arts has wrought. Masters should still be interested in attaining a high level of excellence and should continue in that direction. To extend the pathway analogy a little further, imagine that the white belts are wandering through a field of grass, just starting out. They have been told, and expect to find, that somewhere in that field they will encounter a path that begins to climb through the woods and up the mountain. They wander here and there looking for a sign and hopefully noticing the wildflowers among the grass. They don't linger though, because they know that they are looking for a path that isn't in this part of the field. Masters on the other hand, in their continued travels, find themselves again in this field or one much like that of their beginnings in the martial arts. They aren't concerned about the location of the path; their objective is to visit and examine closely every wildflower and every variety of grass, and they will move things aside to peer at what may be hidden underneath. Such is their interest and joy in details; they revel in the opportunity to study what they may have passed by in their earlier haste. White belts may come upon masters sitting in the grass, chewing on clover or counting the petals of a daisy and think them odd. Seeking direction from the masters will frustrate the white belts who want to be pointed toward their objective and have no plan to tarry with those who are clearly not managing their time well or perhaps have gone a little crazy. The white belts wonder: Do they not know how the world works? Have they wasted everything they have learned? Shouldn't they be showing everyone the places where they have been?

© Revista Sensei

Self-improvement should be the goal of all martial artists regardless of age or ability.

Pursuing Your Goals

The Masters Kiai, like all the Kiai, has many choices built into it, and the masters know full well their responsibility to make good ones. They also know that they must make the decisions that are right for them and that not everyone will like them or approve of them. They must, however, deconstruct their premises and reevaluate what they have learned. This is true even if it means going off in a completely new direction or retreating to a cave in the woods as Miyamoto Musashi (a 17th-century samurai famous for his swordsmanship and arguably the most popular author in the martial arts) did. If the Masters Kiai does not allow this, when else in the training process can it occur?

It is difficult for a student to find a good teacher, but it is more difficult for a master to find a good student. People come to the training with varying objectives, and sometimes it is more important for them to follow their own agendas than those of the teacher. It is not uncommon for senior students to depart from the ways of their teachers, either to explore their own Masters Kiai or because their teachers are pursuing theirs. Those who have given time from their training to help others along the way must take care to ensure that their own progress continues. It is not enough to stand still and direct others, no matter how rewarding and educational that role can be. The masters will, from time to time, need to do more research and testing within their own development, not just through their students or even the teachers who have gone before them.

The nature of the relationship of mind and body will shift and evolve many times during the course of the training. The advanced students who have seen this happen before and have rolled with the changes will be less frightened or confused when confronted with an unexpected plateau or the chaos of a windstorm. Sometimes seniors who are content to enjoy the clean air of a high mountain meadow do not want to engage the self-examination of the Masters Kiai and will fight against any suggestion of descending again or strolling close to the edge where they might fall off.

It is in this way that the training process never ends. Martial artists feel that they are beginning again much of the time, even when it is clear that they are moving forward. All the Kiai have kinetic energy, and the Masters Kiai has more than the rest. The mind and the body are united with such an intensity that when something is out of balance or the integration of component elements is not right, the effect is noticeable. If the master does not correct it, the result can be disturbing.

Acknowledging Limitations

The Masters Kiai, although accepting of change, is not complacent about maintaining harmony or correcting wrongs. One misconception about the equanimity of the masters is that they are never wrong, never lose their grip, and always have the strength to remain calm and collected. This is an unrealistic expectation for masters to have of themselves or for students to have of their teacher. Although it is true that this disturbance will occur infrequently, you must remember that the masters are not perfect, will never be, and that their learning process continues. Also remember that the body will occasionally fail, accidents will happen, and sometimes circumstances in the universe spin out of the control of any individual. The abilities of the Masters Kiai, however, should allow the martial artist to recover quickly and build anew.

Martial artists must guard against allowing these expectations of equanimity to act as a trap or as handcuffs. For self-defense purposes, they must be aware that an opponent can strategically manipulate this situation to force the master into inaction. If the opponent expects the master not to fight back regardless of the provocation or the importance of what needs to be defended, then abuse can occur. The Masters Kiai will use the full range of resources to redirect such an attack, but sometimes the master must simply block a punch or return it. We hope the master will know when there truly is no other way. It is also easy for the advanced students, teachers, or masters to create a cage for themselves in which they are afraid of showing error.

Teaching Only What You Know

Part of the lesson of the Masters Kiai is to not attempt to teach more than what you are confident that you know. This does not suggest holding back knowledge to make it more precious or to appear secretive, rather the Kiai demands that you know a lot about what you are teaching. Examine it with rigor and observe the reactions and responses of the students to what and how you teach. Be willing to admit when you do not know something or are not sure, but work immediately to find the answer through research, contemplation, or consultation with another teacher.

Respecting the Art

We take the tradition of teaching in the martial arts seriously. On a simple level, teaching evolves as one student reaches out to help another and increases as one becomes more senior in the progression. The role of sensei, however, is set apart, because of the commitment to leadership, knowing that others will follow. The responsibility to teach rather than merely instruct in the process is a subtle form of recognition from both parties—the teacher and students—that a special relationship is forming. There must be loyalty to the material and how to teach it, especially when teachers pass on what their teachers taught them. The title of sensei is not given or taken lightly. It is more than what the black belt represents and certainly more than what a championship trophy can suggest. Some are all too quick to call themselves experts or masters at this or that to reassure their potential students and remind their actual students of their abilities. This is understandable in light of the economic climate of making a living or operating a school where people can train. However, the Masters Kiai should not allow students of martial arts who are still intent on learning and improving to take themselves too seriously.

Students should respect their teachers, and teachers should respect the traditions of the arts they are teaching. The teachings are the legacy transmitted by many teachers who worked hard to learn and pass on an important body of knowledge. Be humble; know that the conclusions you draw may not be unique or even correct in the great scheme of things. Too much self-aggrandizement and not enough practice gets in the way of the training.

For the serious martial artist, attaining the black belt should not be exaggerated in importance either before or after. For anyone who has been there,

Students should respect their teachers, and teachers should respect the art and recognize the importance of the role they've been given.

it truly is a new beginning. It looms brightly as a goal from far away and again as you near it. Once achieved, it certainly conveys meaning and responsibility to those who wear it and others who see it. In the Masters Kiai, the dirty white belt is brought down to the river occasionally to be washed, the cup emptied a little and refreshed. To be open to new experiences along the way, a martial artist should not proceed too full or burdened with baggage. Once you have learned to travel lightly, then by all means travel farther and enjoy it.

Realistically Assessing Ability

A teacher may not yet be a master, and a master may not currently be teaching. Not all who open a school or conduct a class in a community center are masters of the martial arts, even if they wear black belts. This does not mean that you should not give them respect, but sometimes people expect too much of them. They may be keen to start a group so they can continue their own training, spread the word, and pass on some benefits they have obtained by participating in the martial arts. We properly attribute the title of sensei, *roshi*, *kenshi*, master, chief poobah, and so on, only to senior people with the background and experience appropriate to the title. This is as much a benefit for those who do not yet feel ready for the mantle, but wish to teach and help out, as it is for those who unwittingly find themselves at the door of the dojo expecting Miyagi sensei from the movie *Karate Kid* or Kwai Chang Caine from the television show *Kung Fu*.

Prospective students of the martial arts should check the credentials of the teachers at the school they are interested in but it is important to remember that in most systems, attaining rank does not necessarily guarantee the ability to teach. It is also true that standards vary considerably from association to association. Further, the fact that someone may not have a pedigree from an elite organization does not mean they are less in value. Remember that these large international schools and associations are formulated primarily for tournament competition, and their internal politics reward artists who train that way. Teachers who do not wish to participate will not find their place among them. There are qualifed individuals who have pursued their paths in the martial arts in other ways. They may be self-taught or have learned from a variety of teachers.

There is no standard in the martial arts, and although it may be confusing for the outsider, we generally consider it a good thing, because it allows differences of opinion and permits a range of approaches for learning the arts. Prospective students will have to examine carefully the options available to them if wishing to study a martial art. It will depend on what is available in the community and what you hope to achieve from it. You shouldn't necessarily go for the school that is closest or has the most trophies in the window. Sometimes you get lucky and find that a good teacher is conducting the class at the local Y. The best advice is to look around, ask questions of the teachers and other students, and listen with an open heart and a discerning mind. Mastery can come in many forms, and the introductory lessons from masters can be most valuable, especially if they hand you a wildflower. There are many doorways into the martial arts, and they swing both ways. Having respect for the Masters Kiai before you begin will go a long way toward setting you on the right path.

Integrating Mind, Body, and Spirit

The Masters Kiai is not about the complete mastery of the mind over the body or the body over the mind. One quality of a master is the ability to compensate for the weakness or inability in one by the directed use of the other. If the integration network is strong and well prepared by the activation of the other Kiai, then it does not matter which is more in control. Ideally, at this level it is the spirit that will drive and unite the energies to survive and achieve. A spirit in harmony, wa, will deal with the challenges, come what may, and will use whatever aspects—mental, physical, or both—are appropriate for the situation. With the Masters Kiai students can recognize disturbances for what they are and isolate themselves a little bit from them. If students keep things in perspective and remember difficulties they have met and overcome before, the mind, body, and particularly the spirit will not be overwhelmed.

Stress, either sudden or repetitive, can produce panic and anxiety in the mind and strong psychological responses that can be damaging. Evidence suggests that these mind-body relationships play a considerable role in disease formation, especially cancer and cardiological weaknesses. It is now commonly accepted in Western medicine that controlling stress and using positive reimaging can dramatically affect the healing process. In Eastern health practices where the mind-body relationship is fundamental, the healthy circulation of ki without distraction or blockage keeps people healthy. Someone who has become ill needs this essential circulation restored.

The Masters Kiai recognizes that a clean, calm wa is a priority, even in the event of stormy weather. Martial artists may reach for the tools of the mind such as visualization or quiet meditation to achieve this or, depending on the circumstances, may rely on the physical processes. Going for a run in the woods will challenge the senses, reoxygenate the blood, burn out toxins from the tissues, and result in clearing the mind. Martial artists can then bring an essential spirit to work on a problem. Stripped to the soul in this way, their appreciation of simple beauty is direct and becomes amplified by rejuvenating the spirit and activating ki energy. This occurs both within the organism and without in the universe and is an undeniable secret of the martial arts. People in other sports and artistic endeavors will have experienced a similar union of energy that places the mind and the body in the same paradigm. The difference is that usually they discover this as an aside or a by-product of the other activity, whereas in the martial arts it is a principal objective. The activity becomes a method for achieving this union. The Kiai of the martial arts, as we have identified them in these chapters, help to codify and explain the experience, not in a linear progression but as various windows into the process.

Reaching Beyond the Masters Kiai

The Masters Kiai is not the ultimate goal of martial arts training. Once students achieve this level, they have all the basic abilities to start learning and doing what the arts have to offer. This is an important point about the black belt; it is like the high school diploma that permits you access to further learning. It is also like acquiring the facility to produce scales and arpeggios on a musical instrument, so you are finally ready to play any piece of music set in front of you or to make up one on your own.

It is not enough to attain this level of practice, then stop. Every day the Masters Kiai is working toward improving, refining, and raising the bar of excellence. Masters are not content to revel in past glory or to teach only what they have already learned. There are many blanks to fill, rough edges to smooth, and new green shoots to reach out with in the Masters Kiai.

There is a universality to the Masters Kiai. It can be anyplace, any time, and everywhere, both within the formal training and in daily life. This is why it is so important to the system to keep the various Kiai always present and in a dynamic balance. Too much emphasis or complacency in one area and the framework grows with weakened links. Dwelling for too long in the Competitive Kiai or Meditative Kiai, for example, brings different results but does not lead to the balanced ecology of the Masters Kiai.

The Super Kiai

The Masters Kiai is not concerned with just integrating the mind with the body. It is more interested in coordinating all those aspects of the training that unite the mind and body throughout all the Kiai. It is the super Kiai, not in a hierarchical sense, but in its completeness as a network that has grown and infiltrated every avenue of energy flow. This circulation and depth make the connection strong and allow sufficient feedback to keep it in balance. It is simply a richer harvest.

Learning

Love of the arts
Expectations
Acquisition
Remember
Nurture
Interest
Nyuanshin
Growing

Training

Tolerance
Regularity
Attitude
Improvement
Neutrality
Interest
No nonsense
Guts

Action

Adaptability
Concentration
Timing
Intelligence
Oneness
Natural

Competitive

Courtesy
Optimism
Mental focus
Perseverance
Enthusiasm
Temporary
Intelligence
Technique
Integrity
Vigilance
Effort

Meditative

Moon
Energy
Delightful
Inspiration
Timeless
Awareness
Transcendental
Intuition
Vibration
Elemental

Master

Mentor
Accessible
Spontaneous
Technique
Energy
Return

Preparing for the Next Climb

Advanced students can become convinced that they have discovered some secret or shortcut when they rise from a plateau to take on the next slope of the training. A tournament result, a change in training technique, or a meditative satori experience can be the trigger or a catalyst for change or improvement, but in most cases it is all the work students do on the plateau that prepares them for the next climb. Inevitably, the only secret to the martial arts remains practice, practice, practice.

"Chance favors the prepared mind," it is said. We find this true in the martial arts, and we follow it with the addendum, "Action favors the prepared body." The martial artist will work hard to sow a field and wants to be there, ready, at the right moment to reap its harvest.

The student with Masters Kiai has learned to accept and enjoy the circularity of all things. The martial arts teach that, although the shortest distance between two points may be a straight line, that isn't always the fastest or most effective way of getting there. Whether you are talking about a long-distance journey or the trajectory of a quick jab to a vulnerable target, the principle is the same. There are lessons from nature and results from daily practice that demonstrate repeatedly that the way is simple, but understanding it is complex. Explaining it can be a different matter entirely. Although you can lead students through the various steps and help them along the way, to explain to someone who is not taking the steps and hope that the explanation is complete or even useful is difficult. In this case especially, the knowing is in the doing. Preparing the mind without the full participation of the body does not achieve the union the martial artist is looking for. It is not enough for the mind to influence and control the body. There are strong physical prerogatives that the body must convey to the mind and that you must incorporate in and around thought structures in order for you to make the most of the partnership. The spirit must be the power plant and convey the important ties that allow the relationship to function, but at the same time the spirit receives the benefits and joys that result therein.

Restoring Natural Balance

Perfection is a thing of dreams, and it may be that we attain it only in passing. We glimpse it in moments in nature; and as beings in nature, we must have it within ourselves as well. A flower, we believe, is unaware of its beauty. It knows success of a sort if it propagates and continues. Its purpose is to take its place in nature and just be, alive and well and struggling with the whims of its environment. It is doubtful that human existence is much more than that in the great scheme of things, although we try hard not to believe so. The scars on the planet that we have collectively left in our passing do not prove our importance; rather they are evidence of our inability to wield the tools of intelligence, choice, invention, and organization that we have developed or been granted by some higher power through evolution.

It is our belief that mastering the martial arts is of little use if not to improve and fortify our connection with the environment. The purpose of modern martial arts should be to further the progression away from things warlike and destructive, and to channel these powerful energies into areas that produce and restore natural balance. In the same way that other biological communities sometimes turn on each other and pollute their nests when they are overcrowded or subjected to stresses to which they have not adapted, the human organism has not yet got it right. We do not seem to realize our potential collectively or individually, mentally or physically. If we are using only a small percentage of our mental capacity, if the physical resources both within our bodies and on our planet are decayed or corrupted, if a few control most of the wealth, then what is going on? How far have we come, and where do we get off alleging our superiority over other beings on the Earth? We can barely master ourselves.

The next great evolution will not be technical if we can't catch up to it in our minds and if we turn away from emotions and physical experiences that enrich us and keep our biological organisms healthy. We must consolidate our intrinsic understanding of our way of being as individuals on this planet to protect what is vital and provide for our continued survival. The greatest threat to us as martial artists is not the fellow in the next village with the sword (although in many communities around the world this is still quite a threat) but a society that is increasingly out of control, disconnected, un-

© Roxanne Standefer

Mastery of the martial arts should be used to improve and fortify our connection with the environment.

healthy, a little crazy, often unhappy, and that continues to pollute the water we drink and the air we breathe.

It is not enough to breathe, relax, and smile when something is wrong. However, it is useful to identify the state in which that maxim is sufficient for health and happiness. Martial artists learn that practicing helps to restore the center of their energy and orient their internal compass sufficiently in that direction until they can figure out what they can do to improve the situation. Acting from that truth, they have power, clarity, unity, and enjoyment.

Martial artists may ask themselves to what use they can put the knowledge, training, and experience they have accumulated. Those in any field who have worked long and hard and have devoted considerable time to an endeavor want some tangible outcome beyond their own development. They might apply what they have learned directly by teaching it to others, and that, of course, benefits the activity as a whole and improves the teacher. Most martial artists also recognize that applying their skills in areas completely outside their technique is extremely productive and satisfying. By translating training principles, philosophical attitudes, and the focus of energy into other kinds of action, they can accomplish great things.

Self-improvement, community development, and the resulting changes that can occur globally reflect the principle of small steps. Acting progressively and cooperatively, we can achieve much larger, seemingly impossible goals. It is up to individuals to decide how to apply themselves to the tasks at hand.

Mind and Body Kiai

Many martial artists have transcended the word "martial" by applying what they have learned in their training to other activities that have no connection, historical, traditional, or otherwise, to anything warrior-like. Martial artists are very peaceful people and although one can easily justify the usefulness of self-defense skills in the modern world, it would be nice to think that in the evolution of the martial arts there could come a time when "martial" is not the best modifying word for the arts. What these arts have offered us is a method of learning about the relationship of the mind and body and a way of directing that energy, that kiai, toward any effort of excellence. When you can bring the intensity, determination, focus, and endurance, as well as the serenity, balance, quiet, and yielding of a true master of martial arts to another activity, you have achieved the purpose of the Mind and Body Kiai.

If we are to accept our responsibilities as humans that have been somehow "blessed" with the ability to reason, invent, and explore new worlds, it is about time that we began to live up to our billing. Within the individual there is great capacity to control what and how we think, and also to create a positive energy. When this energy is fueled by the physical resources of the body in a healthy way, there is potential for elevation of the human condition. Our complex organism is simply ours, we know no other, nor can we feel what another feels. By owning it, fine-tuning it, and expressing our energy with clarity and focus, we can offer the best of ourselves to the world. There is satisfaction to be found in the sense of moving forward with purpose, knowing that you belong in the universe. A healthy body and a healthy mind working together seems right and natural.

The martial arts are a time-tested method of simple steps to get in shape, have fun, and unify the body and the mind. Cultivating your spirit and directing your energy toward self-improvement will facilitate happiness and greatness and give you the strength to roll with the punches. The martial arts embody a philosophy and ethical program that works against the misdirection or abuse of the powers contained in the teachings. Although martial arts may not stop the flood, they can provide humans with the tools to build an ark. One way to do so is to learn to breathe, relax, and smile. There are others. We want to continue to call the martial arts the kind of arts that build healthy individuals and prosperous societies. The martial aspect is not a predominantly destructive tool but one that we can use for rebuilding and recreating the self, in the manner of a sculptor who takes parts away from the block to discover the inner beauty of the marble. The nature of the individual appears when authenticity in personal expression is consistent and genuine.

Applying the Masters Kiai

Never forget your Learning Kiai.

- Accept your accomplishments; enjoy them but don't take yourself too seriously.

- Teach whenever you can. Teach to improve your student, not to show off your abilities. The rewards will be great, and you will continue to improve.

- Allow yourself to make mistakes when trying something new or reexamining what you have known for a long time. Avoid the pitfall of practicing only what you know.

- Use the harmony and integrity you have developed in your high level of activity, and seek to expand it to all areas of your life. Improve your community.

- Take responsibility for your progress. Respect yourself and your students and especially remember those who have gone before. Respect the traditions, teachers, and masters who have contributed knowledge and experience.